AMERICAN PAINTED TINWARE

A Guide To Its Identification

VOLUME ONE

by Gina Martin and Lois Tucker

Caroline
Hope you enjoy
the book.
Lois Tucker

A PUBLICATION OF THE
HISTORICAL SOCIETY OF EARLY AMERICAN DECORATION, INC.

Cover: Decorated tin trunk (circa 1820) from the Stephen North shop in Fly Creek, NY. Part of the
Historical Society of Early American Decoration's collection of artifacts, research material, and
patterns at the Museum of American Folk Art, Two Lincoln Square, New York, NY 10023-6214.

This book has been so long in the making that many people have been involved. Everyone has been helpful in his or her own way, encouraging, constructively criticizing, performing the myriad tasks of publication, writing and proofreading, and all the other jobs, large and small. But throughout the entire effort my husband, Sherwood, has not only been the tireless chauffeur, but more importantly, has been the anchor, doing what anchors do: holding us centered around the prime purpose of the book.

To Sher, therefore, this book is dedicated.

—*Gina Martin*

The Authors:

GINA MARTIN has spent 50 years studying American tinware and more recently seeking a means to positively identify the early American tinshops. She has thousands of photographs of more than 2000 pieces, thus documenting the characteristics in great detail. Mrs. Martin has applied to this field the research techniques of the fine arts historian in authenticating an old master.

Mrs. Martin is a charter member of the Historical Society of Early American Decoration. She served as a judge for several years and also as the Chairman of the Standards and Judging Committee. She is a Master Craftsman, one of the first group so certified by the Society. She was instrumental in developing both the HSEAD School Program and the Teacher Certification Program, and she is herself a Master Teacher. Mrs. Martin also served for several years on the Board of Trustees of the Society.

LOIS TUCKER has had an avid interest in American painted tinware for over 20 years. She began learning the art of duplicating this technique in 1973 and became a Society member in 1976. Her many years in the antique business afforded her access to hundreds of original pieces in the hands of dealers and collectors. Studying, recording, and photographing these originals, as well as those in museums or at auction houses, has allowed her to amass a large file for research.

Mrs. Tucker received her Teacher Certification in Country Painting in 1985 and in Stencilling in 1987. She has served on several committees for the Society, and is currently a member of the Standards and Judging Committee. She is the instructor for the HSEAD School Program for Country Painting. Mrs. Tucker received the Society's Specialist Award for Country Painting in 1994.

The Publisher:

HISTORICAL SOCIETY OF EARLY AMERICAN DECORATION, INC: A society with affiliated chapters organized to carry on the work and honor the memory of Esther Stevens Brazer, pioneer in the perpetuation of Early American Decoration as an art; to promote continued research in that field; to record and preserve examples of Early American Decoration; to maintain such exhibits and publish such works on the subject of Early American Decoration and the history thereof as will further the appreciation of such art, and the elevation of the standards of its reproduction and utilization.

> The Historical Society of Early American Decoration, Inc.
> c/o Beverly McCarthy, Administative Assistant
> 61 West 62nd Street, 3rd Floor
> New York, NY 10023-7015

Table of Contents
Volume I

Foreword . . . .*ix*

Preface . . . . *xi*

Acknowledgements . . . .*xiii*

Introduction . . . . *xv*

18th Century Tin Centers: Map . . . .*xvi*

Historical Perspective *by Shirley DeVoe* . . . . *xviii*

Areas of Early Tin Businesses in Connecticut: Map . . . .*xx*

Chapter One:
The First Tinshops (Berlin CT area) 1
     by Lois Tucker

    Berlin and East Berlin CT: Map 15

    Characteristics of Berlin Area Decoration 20
        by Lois Tucker

        Group I 20

        Group II 28

        Group III 35

        Group IV 48

Chapter Two:
Upson Shop, Marion, Connecticut 55
        by Mona D. Rowell & Lois Tucker

    Characteristics of Upson Shop Decoration 67
        by Gina Martin & Lois Tucker

Chapter Three:

North Shop, Fly Creek, New York 81
> by Mona D. Rowell & Lois Tucker

> Characteristics of North Shop Decoration
> by Gina Martin & Lois Tucker
>> Group I 88
>> Group II 102
>> Group III 109

Chapter Four:

Butler Shop, Greenville, New York 117
> by Mona D. Rowell

> Characteristics of Butler Shop Decoration 131
> by Gina Martin & Lois Tucker

Appendices by Lois Tucker
> APPENDIX A: Checklist For Tinshop Identification 141
> APPENDIX B: Berlin Tinner's Pricing Agreement 144
> APPENDIX C: Pattison & Peck Mercantile Inventory 146
> APPENDIX D: Tinware Items of R. & B. Wilcox Co 147
> APPENDIX E: Tinware Items of John Hubbard 147
> APPENDIX F: Berlin Area Tinners and Peddlers 148
> APPENDIX G: Glossary 152

Bibliography 154

Index 156

VOLUME II
Tinshops of Stevens Plains, Maine

VOLUME III
Filley Tinshops of Connecticut, New York and Pennsylvania

VOLUME IV
Miscellaneous and Unknown Tinshops

FOREWORD

Many books and articles have been written over the years concerning the work done by tradesmen such as the Blacksmith, the Coppersmith and the Tinsmith. It is rare to find any material on the artistic phases of these trades.

Itinerant artists and portrait painters very often did not include a signature on their works. As more and more research has been done, we have learned to identify the works of numerous artists through repeated details and paint usage. The turn of the nose or a detail of the eye becomes as genuine a signature as the man's name on the painting itself.

Returning to the tinsmith's artist, we have learned to identify certain details and, as with the portrait painter, now we can attribute certain signs to real people and areas. Certain structured details and forms are now identified with different areas: one detail is from New England and another from New York or Pennsylvania. Great strides have been accomplished through thorough research.

We also recognize that not only do forms change but painted decoration also changes. Again, in general, we know that New York decorations are different from Maine and from Connecticut. The next step is to study the painted details and to find if it is possible to say this is the work of one artist or that it is by some other hand.

Mrs. Martin has taken this all-important step. She has made an excellent and exhaustive study of the products of the important tinshops. Having studied, photographed and recorded untold numbers of patterns and designs, we can say that the work of several tinshops is now identifiable. It is very possible that more than one member of the families worked or painted these designs. There certainly was one person, however, who taught or controlled the work. In the Upson Shop, for example, there is even a signature (which does not appear on all pieces). It is not a name, but a wonderful tiny face with dots for eyes; but most certainly a signature. It is possible that this is the master's work. Undoubtedly, even as Michelangelo had, there were students and helpers. In another instance, the Buckley Shop, there is a different signature.

This is the first comprehensive study of the tinsmith artist. It most certainly is hoped that Mrs. Martin or others will be inspired to extend this type of study and knowledge until an Index of Tinsmith Painting Artists may be completed.

Henry J. Harlow
Curator (1957–1979)
Old Sturbridge Village

Preface

It is the purpose of this book to provide the information, characteristics, and identifying features that will enable the student of painted tinware to identify the shop where a piece was decorated. As the interest in American folk art has escalated in recent years, the need for verifying the authenticity of those items has similarly increased. The serious buyer wants to acquire a proven item and not just a piece that appears to be like some other object. Although some areas of folk art have already been reasonably documented, American painted tinware has not. It is hoped that this book will introduce a scholarly and rational approach for identifying decorated tinware, not just to geographical areas but to the tinshop in which the article was produced. It will no longer be necessary to call an item merely New England, New York, or Connecticut but to identify the object as being from a specific tinshop.

Beginning collectors and students of painted tinware will find herein ample examples and detailed illustrations to enable them to make these identifications. This book will guide them through the necessary steps by starting the identifying process with a known piece, and calling attention to additional distinctive features with each succeeding example. Experienced collectors and advanced students will find multiple examples of known tinware and will be able to hone more finely their skills of identification.

The painted characteristics which will be illustrated and referred to are usually best displayed on the fronts of trunks. In some instances the design on the end or top of the trunk will provide the distinguishing characteristics when the trunk front has a design in which similarities to more than one shop are found. For example, in the North shop, the unique three-quarter striping on the end of a trunk is a defining feature. The student is urged to become familiar with trunks first, and then to use that knowledge to classify other types of pieces. The various motifs used in creating the design [flowers, leaves, borders, etc.] should be carefully studied and their correlation to the major design recognized.

Identification of an Unknown Item

The approach to identification should first be made from the overall decoration. The fronts of trunks and the major display areas of waiters, canisters and bread baskets provide the feeling that experienced students have when they first view a piece. It is probably a subconscious application of the knowledge of characteristics gained through examining many pieces. Beginners will develop this over time and the feeling is merely a starting point. There are often such similarities between shops, however, that the overall design might not give an immediate positive identification. It will then be necessary to look for clues in the individual motifs or sometimes in the relationships among the several sections of the object, such as the peculiar North striping mentioned above. Distinction between painters can be shown in the simplest brushstrokes by the thickness of the paint, the shapes, and even the direction of the stroke. The shapes of flowers, fruits, berries and leaves are often the unique feature. The presence and execution of borders and bands, whether straight, curved, or scalloped, provide further differences. Obviously, the more characteristics which can be found, the more secure the identification to a particular tinshop becomes.

The reader should refer to the checklist in Appendix A for help in the tinshop identification process.

TÔLE OR TÔLEWARE (a misnomer)

It has become the practice of antique dealers, auction houses, and the public in general to refer to this painted tin as tole or toleware. Tôle is the French word for sheet iron and the term is correctly used to denote heavy gauge iron trays and other metalware items produced and decorated in France during the 18th century. Tôle often had background colors of dark green, ivory, dark red, or black.

The term tole does not correctly apply to the American tinplated sheet iron (or English tinplated ware). Our tinware should be referred to as either 'American painted tinware,' 'japanned ware,' or simply 'country painted tin'.

ACKNOWLEDGEMENTS

The completion of this first volume could not have been accomplished without the help of many people, each with greatly varied interests in the subject of painted tinware. Some are decorators themselves and are keeping alive for future generations this nearly lost art from past generations. Some are museum curators or personnel who are preserving many wonderful examples of the nineteenth century decorated tin. Some are private collectors who satisfy their love of this art by living daily with their antique pieces adorning their cupboards and shelves. Some are the dealers in the antique trade who spent many hours searching down pieces and then passing them along to the collectors. All have their own particular reasons for being interested in decorated tin, and all have been helpful to the authors.

Our appreciation is given to Mona D. Rowell for her invaluable work on the history texts in the Upson, North and Butler chapters. Mrs. Rowell's service to the Historical Society of Early American Decoration over the years has been remarkable. She was a member of the Board of Trustees for eighteen years and served four years as President. She has been curator of the HSEAD Museum at Cooperstown, director of the HSEAD school program, and editor of *The Decorator*. She also conducted seven study tours to Europe. Mrs. Rowell is a certified teacher in country painting, stencilling, and Pontypool painting. She has also been a member of the Exhibition, Judging, and Teacher Certification committees.

The first tinshop to be researched was the Upson shop. Tremendous help was given by Avis Heatherington, who first suggested the use of illustrative drawings to help tie together and prove the various shop characteristics. Madge Watt and Astrid Donnellan were also invaluable with their support. Additional thanks go to Betty Montgomery, Evelyn Tuffin, Helen Butler, Liz Church, and Gail Woodard. Maryjane Clark must be included for her generosity in sharing photographs of originals. Her support and knowledge have been of extraordinary benefit to the authors.

Many have helped by doing research, taking photographs, or visiting museums in their areas for the authors. A special appreciation for their efforts goes to Jane Bolster, Flo Lewis, Lucinda Perrin, Helga Johnson, Barbara Upson and Kathleen Hutcheson.

A vast amount of help has been proffered from museums and this also is appreciated. Anne C. Golovin, curator of the Division of Social History, and Jennifer Oka, Museum Specialist, both of the Museum of Natural History, Smithsonian Institution, have been most helpful with information on their tinware collection. Kay Gurske, curator of the Berlin Historical Society, has been most generous in helping, as have

David and Ann Borthwick, Berlin historians. A very special thanks goes to Donald Fennimore, Curator of Metals at Winterthur, who spent an entire day helping Lois photograph pieces in the museum's collection. He was most generous with his time and the museum's files on tinware. Douglas White of the Ohio Historical Society, Gail M. Getz of the State Museum of Pennsylvania, and the late Henry Harlow at Old Sturbridge Village have also been of tremendous help.

Private collectors and antique dealers who have generously allowed their collections and stock to be studied have proved to be an invaluable help. Special thanks are given to Lewis W. Scranton (Antiques), Pat Hatch (Harvard Antique Shop), the late Molly Porter, Orrin C. Stevens, Martha S. Vernlund, Alice Nutting Vincent (York Antique Gallery), William F. Graham (Graham's Antiques), and all the various members of the Historical Society of Early American Decoration who through the years have brought their original tinware pieces to the national meetings to be photographed and studied.

These acknowledgements cannot be completed without a very special thanks to Donald Tucker, Lois' husband. He guided her through the manipulations of the computer, and its capabilities for use with this project. He has offered many suggestions that have helped to keep the book from becoming so technical that the novice would not be able to understand it. He has proofread, corrected, and rearranged sentence structure, as well as helped with the layout of the illustrative drawing sections. This project might never have been completed without his guidance.

To produce a comprehensive reference book, it is necessary for the writers to search every possible avenue where additional knowledge of the subject may be gained. This is never possible without the help and assistance of other people, and we thank each and every one of them. Without the efforts of all those involved, the first volume of *American Painted Tinware* could not have reached fruition.

gm & lt

INTRODUCTION

PHOTOGRAPHS

In choosing the photographs to be used in this book, a number of criteria had to be considered. The foremost of these was the presence of a distinguishing characteristic that fit within the sequence which follows the step-by-step progression from the first attributed piece through to the end. The photographs of original tinware represent fifty years of researching under all types of circumstances. Many pieces of tinware have been found at auction houses, antique shows, garage sales, flea markets, and other places that were not conducive to excellent photographic conditions. Throughout the book, the best photographs have been used to illustrate a particular characteristic. Tinware that is in the best condition has been used whenever possible.

LINE-DRAWN ILLUSTRATIONS

The drawings presented within this book are very detailed. Abbreviating these illustrative keys was for a time considered, but often only the most detailed study of a piece, and examination of all characteristics, can lead to an identification.

Each illustration has been drawn to scale, but that scale may vary from one drawing to the next. No attempt has been made to size each piece with its neighbor. The reader should use each drawing as a study for painted details only. Many of the antique pieces (especially trunks) from which these drawings were taken are now bent and mishapen. The drawings may reflect this.

All brushstrokes, dots, and other details demonstrated as solid black areas denote work painted on the original tinware with yellow pigment. Red, green, and all other colors are not separately distinguished. Units or strokes originally painted in any color other than yellow are illustrated merely as line drawings.

Painted bands have been shaded in the illustrations. Many bands, particularly on trunks, have a very complicated form. The shading helps to demonstrate the position of the band, often with an adjoining swag, and eliminate any confusion caused by stripe lines or other features included in the drawings.

Individual characteristics which have been underlined in the written section are considered to be unique to that particular tinshop. These specific strokes or techniques may be used as a single identifying feature for the shop, and very little else may be necessary to confirm the identification. It should be remembered, however, that the more features that can be established with certainty, the stronger the identification becomes.

18th Century Tin Centers

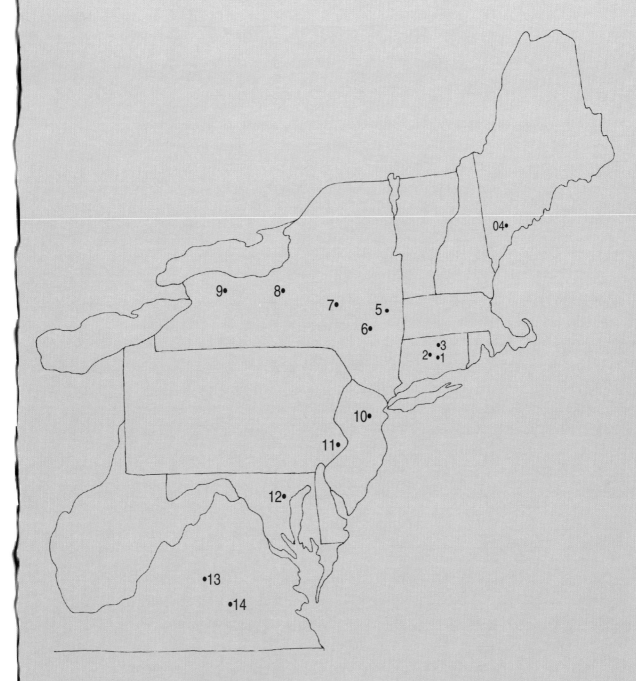

1. Berlin, Connecticut
2. Southington, Connecticut
3. Bloomfield, Connecticut
4. Stevens Plains, Maine
5. Lansingburg, New York
6. Greenville, New York
7. Fly Creek, New York
8. Rome, New York
9. Palmyra, New York
10. Elizabeth, New Jersey
11. Philadelphia, Pennsylvania
12. Baltimore, Maryland
13. Richmond, Virginia
14. Petersburg, Virginia

HISTORICAL PERSPECTIVE

by Shirley Spaulding Devoe

Mrs. Shirley Devoe, who passed away in October 1991, was a student of Esther Stevens Brazer and a charter member of the Historical Society of Early American Decoration. She devoted over forty years to researching and studying the history of the tin industry, both American and English. Her many articles on various phases of the subject appeared in the leading magazines of the period. She was well known for three outstanding books: "The Tinsmiths of Connecticut," "English Paper Maché of the Georgian and Victorian Periods," and "The Art of the Tinsmith, English and American."

THE TIN INDUSTRY IN AMERICA

The production of household tinware was a budding industry in Hartford County, Connecticut before the American Revolution. The business originated with Edward Pattison of Berlin where he settled upon his arrival from northern Ireland about 1740. The date of Pattison's birth is not known, but he died in 1787. His small shop was located on the Hartford and New Haven Path, a much traveled thoroughfare between those two colonies.

For making the tinware Pattison required such raw materials as tinplate, wire and lead which had to be imported from Pontypool, Wales. In the early days these raw materials were obtained in Boston and carted to Berlin by oxcart or by coastal boat, but later New York merchants could also supply the tin shops with these imported materials.

Pattison worked alone at first, accumulating enough of his products to sell from his shop or to peddle around the countryside. His silvery tinware was greatly admired by all because, before its introduction on this side of the Atlantic, the household utensils were of horn, wood, iron and pewter.

The young men of the area saw that business was good so they were eager to learn the trade and Pattison agreed to teach them. Soon most of the homes in Berlin had a trained tinsmith and his apprentices; and so began an industry that was in the next century to involve a large part of the population of Hartford County.

The early tinshops were small and were located in the dooryard of the worker's home, handy to doing his farm chores, because in those days families lived off the land. Pattison taught his apprentices to make what he made, forms that were handed down to their successors from the eighteenth century. Many of the tin utensils were fashioned after practical English pottery and metal wares [pewter and silver], but occasionally a new idea was introduced by a Yankee tinsmith. For example, the tinplate came in sheets measuring 10 inches by 14 inches, so to obtain a larger tray two sheets of tinplate were joined to make a 'seamed waiter'. This was the only large tray of American make until the twentieth century.

PEDDLERS AND TRANSPORTATION

With the increased production of tinware, it became necessary to find a wider market, and men were hired to promote and sell Connecticut products. The peddler was the only means of establishing connections between the manufacturer and the distant consumers, many of whom lived in relatively lonely outposts. There were, it seems, plenty of young adventurous men willing to penetrate the wilderness in aid of commerce. During the first thirty years of the 19th century, half the male population of Hartford County were peddlers, if only for a brief time. Some were tinsmiths who left the bench and tools for the road. One man said: "The devil with the tin" and left for Baltimore. Others went to Canada or, in winter, to the South where they established an agency or depot from which to peddle tinware in the back country. This was a system of marketing that placed their products into every inhabited part of the country at a time when transportation was most primitive. Today this system is considered by many to have been the tinsmith's greatest contribution to American industry and, because of it, Connecticut has held a leading position in the manufacture of metal goods ever since.

About the peddler, P.T. Barnum said: "He was the advertising medium for the tin shop and his wagon a trading post." The intrepid peddler traveled over paths, trails and poor roads, often walking beside his cart or wagon when the roads were very bad in preference to being jolted over the rocks and holes. He progressed from foot to horseback, to a two-wheeled cart, but a four-wheeled wagon, even a springless one, was best for the long distances.

During the first quarter of the nineteenth century the peddler's wagon was the flatbed type, often covered with an arched canvas top. About 1830 this box wagon became the standard vehicle and remained in use for as long as the peddlers worked the country roads. It had hinged sides that lifted to reveal shelves holding tinware. There were also cubbyholes for small items and a large tailgate area in which could be stored the barter. At first these wagons were leather-mounted like the old stage coaches, because steel springs were not invented until 1830. Later in the century the brightly painted box wagon had metal springs.

Land travel was not the only way the peddlers had of reaching the settlements. Braving the wind and waves and avoiding the winter months, the men sailed from a Connecticut River port to New York City. From there they took a coastal vessel bound for Savannah, Mobile or New Orleans where they hoped to exchange tinware for cotton money. The sea voyage was often rough, a circumstance that lengthened the voyage, damaged tinware and caused discomfort to the passengers. In bad weather the trip to New Orleans could take over a month. Upon arrival in the South the peddler would buy a horse and wagon, and then continue up country on a selling trip. At the end of the season he sold the horse and wagon and sailed home to Connecticut.

To transport tinware by sea, barrels and boxes were the containers. They were filled with plenty of sawdust, wood shavings or straw packed around and between the items of tinware to provide the needed protection. After the tinware was carefully packed, it was carted to the nearest wharf and placed on a sailing vessel or later a paddle steamer.

All tin shops handled barter or truck as the country discards were called. It was received in trade for tinware and other goods because in those days the truck was more valuable than money. In 1822 a tinsmith wrote: "I don't take but little cash when I can get truck for it is better than cash. Most of all the truck is in demand; more can be made by having quantities and knowing the market." The bartered goods could be old pewter, brass, linen rags, goose quills, wool, flax, tallow, hair, fur, deerskins, wood ashes, and sometimes an old horse or cow. Once, a communion service was rescued from the back of a peddler's wagon where it had been thrown for barter.

Mink skins brought from twelve to thirty cents each, but prime fox skins were preferred for they were worth a dollar or more. Hen feathers at six cents a pound were in great demand for beds, while the more desirable goose feathers brought the considerable price of seventy-five cents a pound.

When the peddler returned to the shop after a trip, he would unload his barter that was then sorted, counted, weighed and listed with the current market value noted beside each entry. The shop owner then wrote a list of tinware of equal value to the barter and at the bottom of the list: "Rec'd payment by a load of tinware" under which the peddler signed his name.

JAPANNING AND PAINTING

Japanning was the coating of tinware with black and clear varnish. The black varnish was the background coat, and the clear was the medium for painting the design and for the finish coat. Varnish was a substitute for oriental lacquer and was introduced into American tinshops at the end of the eighteenth century. The formulae were brought from England by emigrant artisans and there is evidence that the method used also came from the Pontypool works. By 1810 japanning had become an important part of the American tin industry.

A handwritten receipt for making clear Japann, marked Southington, 1800, was once among the Upson papers and is now in the library of Old Sturbridge Village. With some punctuation for clarity, the document reads: "Take a gallon of linseed oil, one pound of ember [amber] & boil them and strain them. Boil until by putting two knife blades into it and parting them it will draw out in small strings, then put it into bottles and let it stand too or three days & it is for ye use by putting some spirits of turpentine into it. Then it is sufficient to brush on. Sd Japann is to be put on with a brush." For black japan, one-half pound of lamp black was added to one pint of clear varnish. This japan mixture was cooked over an open fire which was a hazardous task for it was highly flammable and often caused serious accidental fires. Later in the nineteenth century the japan was prepared in a separate building called a japan shop.

The coating of tinware with varnish was developed in the 17th century when English artisans were imitating Oriental lacquer. The work was named for the country because the true Japanese product was considered superior to other Eastern lacquers and the English artisans hoped to equal it. That they were successful to a degree we learn from *A Collection of Husbandry and Trade,* 1694, which states: "Japan brought to that perfection not only outdoes all that is made in India, but vies for its lacquer with the Japan[ese] Lacquer itself; and there is hope of imitating its best Draught and Figures." ['India' was also commonly used for Oriental wares and derived from the East India ships that brought them to England.]

Because the population of Connecticut was then mainly English, the industries, methods and expressions of the mother country had been brought here by the settlers and practiced here. It was only natural then that the tinshops began to japan the tin in a modest way at the end of the 18th century. A change from the black background occurred about 1815 when red and blue japanned wares were also made.

The decorative painting provided interesting work for girls and women who liked to paint. Brush control was more important than artistic ability, because the designs were made up of light, quick brushstrokes in great variety. The work of experienced painters had a sureness, a spirited quality and the borders had a flowing continuity. There was a similarity in many of the designs with occasional personal and regional differences. Japanning and ornamenting were to continue industrially through the 19th century but with changes in the method of ornament and production as industrial growth demanded faster methods.

Boys were apprenticed but girls were taught in the shop. The girls also applied the japan, but if a girl wanted to paint, she was given six weeks to learn while japanning the tinware.

At the turn of the century the painting was called flowering, an 18th century term used in the English potteries where the painters were called flowerers. Every New England home had some English earthenware with designs suitable for use on tinware, and so, like their English counterparts, the girls flowered tinware with designs adapted from teapots, pitchers and other dishes. Unfortunately, contemporary documents contain no clear description of the painted designs and it is a rare piece that is signed. But some designs become familiar because of an unusual leaf form or an inventive flower while others are recognized as being from a certain area or shop. These are placed in a separate category until more clear identification can be established.

As both the painters and the peddlers traveled (the painters to work in out-of-state shops and the peddlers to sell), difficulties arise when tinshop identification is attempted. But even with this commercial distribution of the tinware, there has been an encouraging amount of identification of the painter's or shop's designs.

Areas of Early Tin Businesses in Connecticut

(Current town boundaries)

SIMSBURY

WINDSOR

BLOOMFIELD

AVON

WEST
HARTFORD

HARTFORD

BURLINGTON

FARMINGTON

WETHERSFIELD

BRISTOL

PLAINVILLE

NEW
BRITAIN

NEWINGTON

ROCKY
HILL

SOUTHINGTON

BERLIN

CROMWELL

MERIDEN

MIDDLETOWN

MIDDLEFIELD

Chapter One

THE FIRST TINSHOPS
[circa 1740—1850]
Berlin, Connecticut

The origin of tinware manufacture in America is attributed to Edward Pattison. It is impossible today to ascertain how many individual tinshops were operating in the Berlin area. As Edward Pattison trained the local men in the trade, they in turn took on apprentices to learn the tin business. This process continued, multiplied, and produced untold numbers of tinmen working within this area of Connecticut. The identity of the vast majority of them is lost in obscurity. Those who had a successful business that lasted for a number of years generally made their mark on the history of Berlin so that some information of their existence and operations can be found in the local records and among archival material.

In 1813 the major tinners in Berlin decided that it was necessary for them to reach an agreement on the pricing of their products. On June 16 a list of the minimum price at which a piece of plain or japanned tinware would be sold was agreed upon by Shubael Pattison, Orin Beckley, Samuel Pattison, John Dunham, Samuel Gilbert, John Goodrich Sr., Aziel Belden, John Buckman, John Hubbard, Benjamin Wilcox, Samuel Kelsey, and Patrick Clark (see Appendix B). Most of these men, as well as a few others, are included in this chapter. The names of other Berlin area men involved in some aspect of the tin industry will be found in Appendix F.

Pattison Family

According to Kenneth Manning Pattison: "In the early 1700s Edward Pattison together with his wife and children fled to Dungannon, County of Tyrone in Northern Ireland to escape the religious and political persecution that was so rampant in his native Scotland. It was his plan to emigrate to the North American colonies. There he planned to use his knowledge of tinware manufacturing to support his family and establish a home for his wife and five children. Unfortunately the mother died shortly after their arrival in Ireland. In 1738 the eldest son Edward journeyed

Connecticut Courant July 9, 1797. Connecticut State Library, Hartford, Connecticut (hereafter CSL).

to Boston and spent some time making enquiries for the family. In his absence tragedy struck again with the death of the father. Returning to Ireland, Edward persuaded his brothers and sisters that opportunities in the colonies would be to their liking. Preparations made and passage purchased, Edward, William, Anna, Noah and Jennie embarked. Landing on the east coast they proceeded overland to the Connecticut Colony and the area now called Berlin." [1]

William worked with Edward in the tin business during the early years, but he eventually turned to blacksmithing in order to make the tools required by the growing number of tinsmiths. [2] He settled first in Wethersfield, then in Kensington, New Britain and Worthington. Berlin itself had been incorporated from these latter three parishes in 1785. William married Sarah Dunham and in later years was rated as one of the wealthiest men in his parish. Edward's sister Anna, who was 16 years old when she emigrated, married Amos Galpin of Berlin in 1745. Noah and Jennie Pattison eventually moved to the southern states.

Edward Pattison established his tinware business soon after his arrival in Berlin. It would seem likely that he brought his supplies with him. The means for a family to make a living in the New World would be a major consideration for any who planned to emigrate. The supplies or necessary tools needed for this livelihood would undoubtedly account for a large part of their freight.

Edward's home was on Hart Street (later named Lower Lane) and his shop, which his neighbors called the Bang-All, was next to the house. In order to sell his wares, he would load his utensils into baskets fitted on his horse, and then travel from house to house in the area. His business grew, and by 1760 he hired other men to help him and to learn the art of the whitesmith. Since the tinplate that Edward used was imported from Great Britain, the Revolutionary War put a temporary halt to Edward's enterprise. Whether or not Edward served in the Revolution is unclear. The muster rolls list both an Edward and a William, but there is no indication as to which Edward and William this is. The names could refer to Edward's and William's sons, who were 17 and 16 years old respectively at the start of the war. The fact that Edward wrote his will in July 1776 might indicate that he planned to serve, if only briefly. During part of the war, he peddled notions such as scissors, thimbles, buttons, pins, combs and brass. [3]

When the war was over, Edward resumed tinsmithing and now hired peddlers to carry the tinware to the South and West. The men Edward had trained were also making tin to be peddled far and wide, as well as training more apprentices themselves. The business became a large enterprise for the town, and was a major factor in the success of Berlin's

[1] Pattison, Kenneth Manning, *Pattison—A Family Chronicle 1480—1992,* p. 23

[2] Ibid., p. 36

[3] Kern, Laura, Berlin Ct: *What Is Special About It?*

becoming a large commercial center for all types of trade common for that period. By the early 1820s, Berlin industries that correlated with the tin business consisted of 12 tinshops, 6 tinner's tools shops, 9 blacksmiths, and 9 carriage and wagon makers. Many other businesses thrived in the town as well: such as cabinet and carpenter shops; clock and watch shops; hat factory; milliner, tailor, and dress shops; cobbler shops; book binderies; tanneries; drug, grocery, dry goods, and general merchandise stores; cider mills; comb maker shop; cooper shop; slaughter house; spectacle maker shop; stove factories; the brandy distillery, taverns and saloons; and a whipping post.

In 1751 Edward Pattison [circa 1720—1787] married Elizabeth Hills [circa 1732—1804]. They had six children: Rhoda [b. 1755], Lucretia [b. 1757], Edward [b. 1759], Lois [b. 1762], Shubael [b. 1764], and Elizabeth [b. 1768]. Edward died in 1787, and his will left his tin business to his two sons. Although we have no record of the types of tinware that Edward produced, his estate inventory does list some items: eight tin canisters, four tin kettles, tin tea kettle, two tin candlesticks, a load of tin, a number of tin patterns, and tinner's tools.

Shubael Pattison [1764—1828] and Edward Pattison Jr. [1759—1809] continued their father's business but it is not known if Edward Jr. remained with his brother for long. He died insolvent and many of the local tinmen were listed among the creditors against his estate. This might imply that he was not a part of his brother's successful business at the time of his death. In 1797 Shubael built a larger shop on the south corner of his land and was advertising under the name of Shubael Pattison and Samuel Porter III. The partnership with Samuel Porter [1762—1818]

The Partnership of
Pattison, Porter & Co.
Is this day by mutual confent, diffolved.
Shubael Pattifon,
Samuel Porter, 3d,
Patrick Clark.
N. B. The bufinefs will be continued at the fame flore by *Pattifon & Porter*, where they have for fale an extenfive affortment of ufeful and fafhionable GOODS, at the moft reduced prices for cafh only.
SHUBAEL PATTISON,
SAMUEL PORTER, 3d.
Berlin, Feb. 16, 1802.

Connecticut Courant Feb. 16, 1802. (CSL).

JACOBITES

During the latter part of the 17th century and first half of the 18th century, Scotland was the focus of conflict between the supporters of the Church of Scotland and those seeking to impose a form of the episcopal church of England. The conflict was exacerbated by those supporting a Protestant monarchy as opposed to those supporting the Catholic monarchy of James II. The supporters of James II were known as Jacobites.

The Protestant Church of Scotland was formed in 1560 by John Knox. The Catholic Mary, Queen of Scots, who became a victim of the religious and political conflict, was forced to abdicate in 1567. She fled to England where she was later executed by Elizabeth I; however, her son James I succeeded Elizabeth I on the English throne in 1603. He and his Stuart descendants (Charles I, Charles II and James II) sought to establish a form of the episcopal church in Scotland but were vigorously resisted by the Church of Scotland

After the Glorious Revolution of 1688-89 in England, the Catholic James II was deposed in favor of his Protestant daughter Mary II and her husband William III. This guaranteed Presbyterianism in Scotland. During the next 50 years the Jacobites continued to try to reestablish the Stuart monarchy. In 1715 when the Hanoverian King George I assumed the English throne after the death of the Protestant Stuart Queen Anne, there was a major uprising by the Jacobites and others in England and Scotland who opposed his rule. They sought to reestablish the Catholic Stuarts but they were defeated in 1716. Again in 1745, there was a final uprising when Charles Stuart (Bonnie Prince Charlie) attempted to raise the clans against the monarchy. He was defeated in 1746, bringing an end to the Jacobite hopes.

During the first half of the 18th century many Jacobites and others caught up in the struggle between the factions fled Scotland for Ireland and eventually America.

lasted until a few years before Samuel's death. Shubael then became associated with his son-in-law, Elisha Peck, who served as proprietor of the general mercantile store. For a time Patrick Clark, a Meriden tinner, had been associated with the Pattison and Porter enterprise. Shubael's business was large and successful; and his peddlers and their wagon loads were even sent into Canada to sell, and to trade for furs. Shubael is said to have been accompanied by John Jacob Astor on some of the Canadian trips. With the furs acquired on these trips, he would hire girls from the Berlin area to make muffs, mittens, and other articles for the store.

In 1787 Shubael married Sarah Hart [1769—1846], the daughter of Zachariah Hart, his father's neighbor. They had ten children, eight of whom survived: Harriet [1788—1847], Chloe [b. 1790], Samuel [b. 1792], Lucy [b. 1794], Ira [1796—1818], Julia [b. 1799], Sarah [b. 1802], and Lois [b. 1807]. His son Samuel and two of his sons-in-law, Elisha Peck and Orin Beckley, were very much involved with Shubael in the business.

Elisha Peck [1789—1851], the son of Elisha and Lucretia (Pattison) Peck, had married his cousin Chloe, daughter of Shubael. He became a partner in his father-in-law's firm and the business was known as Pattison & Peck from about 1815. Elisha moved with his family to New York City about 1820 where he became part of the firm of Phelps, Peck & Co, importers and manufactures of copper, tinplate, and sheet iron.[4] Elisha's account books for the period 1815 to 1818 at the Berlin company are preserved at the Connecticut Historical Society and offer a wealth of information as to what items the store had available for sale. (see Appendix C).

Orin Beckley [1784—1836] , who married Shubael's daughter Harriet in 1812, had been a clerk for the Pattison & Porter business. About the time of the dissolution of that firm, Orin undertook the expansion of the business to Baltimore, Maryland. As the peddling business branched out far from Connecticut, many tinmen were setting up their wintertime business in southern towns. Orin's first wife, Julia Beckley, had died in childbirth in 1808, but when he traveled, Orin remained in contact with her parents. The following letter, in the hands of family descendants, describes the Baltimore business.[5]

Baltimore 4th Febr 1810

Dear Parents.

With pleasure I imbrace this oppertunity to Inform you that I injoy a good state of health at present which I hope is the happy lot of you & the rest of my friends in Berlin. I have not much news at present time with our business hear this winter is verry good wea have been drove for tin verry harde since I have ben hear wea have fifteen to work at tin & five to Jappan & flour tin & wea work upon an average betwint

---

[4] Peck, Ira B., *A Genealogical History of the Descendants of Joseph Peck*, p. 380.

[5] Sheppard, Caroleen Beckley, *The Descendants of Richard Beckley of Wethersfield, Connecticut*, pp. 100—101.

sixty & sevnty boxes a month. I expect wea shall have to work about three hundred boxes more before I shall cum home which will bea about the first of June. It has ben a verry warm winter hear till about two weks since & that has ben verry cold. yesterday wea had a verry great snow which make It look like old fashon winters. I wish you would take the trouble to rite to me & inform me about the times in Berlin this winter & about my friends as I want to hear from you all verry mutch. Please to give my Love to my father and mother my brothers and sisters & all Inquareing friends. this from your ever

Loveing Son Orin Beckley

To David & Eunice Beckley

NB. Please to inform my father that I have resieved both of his Letters.

Shubael conveyed the business to Orin Beckley between 1820 and 1824, at which time Shubael took a mortgage from Orin for $2,800 for the house, store, and other buildings. Chauncey Shipman, who had been involved in the business with Shubael in 1814, was also associated with Orin. Shubael was by then working with Benjamin Wilcox in operating a cotton mill situated on the Mattabesitt River in East Berlin. The cotton was spun into yarn at the mill, and the yarn was then sent out to the local women to be woven into cloth. A letter dated March 1828 by Harriet Pattison Beckley to her sister Chloe Pattison Peck says: "Father is very much engaged in his factory at present he has no time to attend any other business. I sometimes think he will lose all he has in that establishment. I have been informed he does not make the business very profitable. He is old (64) and has not the judgement that he formerly had although he does not think so."[6] Shubael died in November 1828 after becoming suddenly ill while on a trip to New York City. His funeral service in Berlin was the largest the town had ever seen.

Orin Beckley continued to run the store and tinware business until a heart condition forced him to sell his stock to Plumb & Deming in 1830 and to rent out the store for five years. About this time also, Shubael's shop building was moved to the corner and made into a dwelling house. Orin died in 1836, and so ended nearly a century of the Pattison family business in Berlin. It is interesting to consider that Edward Pattison, whom it is said arrived in Berlin with 18¢ in his pocket, started a business that the last owner would eventually sell and leave an estate valued at nearly $12,000.

The tinware manufacturing in Berlin would not come to an end after Orin's death as there were many other whitesmiths who would carry on. And the store itself would continue to serve in the same function for another century, although no longer run by members of the Pattison family. The house and the store burned in 1861, and the store was rebuilt out of

[6] Pattison, Kenneth Manning, *Pattison—A Family Chronicle 1480—1992*, p. 35.

Curious Prank of Recent Hurricane Revealed

October 5, 1938

THE HERALD

brick that same year. The original store had been built in 1797 and from then until 1954 it had been under twenty different ownerships.

The tin business had grown to enormous proportions since Edward had made the first pieces in America. In 1815, 10,000 boxes of tinplate were made into articles.[7] A box of common tin contained 225 sheets of tinplate measuring about 10 x 14 inches. The quantity of scrap tin was enormous, and it would usually be buried in the neighborhood. It was said that several roads in town gave off a silvery ring when a swift team of horses traveled over them. Many fruit trees planted by the locals died because their roots could not penetrate through the tin scraps. In the early 1900s the farmer's plow could still bring up pieces of tin. The hurricane of 1938 toppled a huge maple tree in the Worthington section of town, and various pieces of tinware were ensnared within its roots.

Wilcox Family

The Wilcox family resided in the section of East Berlin—Middletown known in the early days as Upper Houses. Richard, Benjamin, Sylvester and Daniel were the sons of Samuel and Phebe (Dowd) Wilcox. Richard

---

[7] Dwight, Timothy, *Travels in New-England and New-York Vol. II*, p. 45, at State Archives, Connecticut State Library.

and Benjamin were tinners who formed the R. & B. Wilcox Co. They operated their tin business and sent out peddlers, as was the practice among the tinsmiths of the area since Edward Pattison's time. They also set up a wintertime business in Virginia. Although it is unknown at what date they commenced this southern venture, by 1817 Benjamin was in Richmond and Richard was in Petersburg. Their correspondence, preserved by the Berlin Historical Society, tells us something of this venture. For a list of the types of tinware produced by R. & B. Wilcox, see Appendix D.

Benjamin Wilcox [1782—1843] married Betsey Savage [1787—1831] and following are some excerpts from his letters to her:

January 1817: Benjamin replies to a letter from Betsey in which she mentioned his return to Connecticut from Richmond in February. "You wrote further that you felt vary uneasy about our return by water this winter & that the girls were advised not to come by water…You probably are expecting to here something about our business here. I think the prospect is that we shall make a living though our peddlers complain of hard times. I think they do as well as I expect…Our whole company are tolably helthy. Edwin Porter has been very sick, has been unable to do any work for two weeks. I expect Edwin and Norton will return when I do. Also the girls."

December 1818: "Richard has gottn well. Ashbel has got the glanders as bad as Richard had. Edwin has been sick, has lost two days…As for the girls they are real harty. They will begin to Japan this week. They appear to be vary contented."

January 1819: Benjamin hopes to set out for home in February although it is uncertain because "the girls say that they must go with me. They did conclude to stay until Spring once…They are as contented as ever. They had a right smart chance last week to go to the sarcus. Mr. Dickenson & Roxy and Mr. C. Porter & Marilla had the pleasure of going to the sarcus in the snow."

The "girls" mentioned in Benjamin's letters are obviously his decorators. Their full identity is not disclosed, but some speculation can be made. Benjamin's first letter to Betsey also says: "You wrote that Mrs. Roberts had wrote to Roxy. She has not received any. She wants someone to write." We might infer from this that one of the girls is Roxy Roberts, although extensive research into the Roberts families in Connecticut has not yet verified this.

As for Marilla, she may well have been Marilla North [1799—1872], daughter of Levi and sister to Jedediah and Edmund North, owners of J & E North Manufacturing Co., makers of tinman's tools. In a letter by Albert North of Fly Creek, NY (see Chapter 3 for North Tin Shop), he writes to his first-cousin Jedediah and suggests that he send one of his sisters saying "I think that I can occupy her Leisure hours at Painting."[8] This letter would

Wilcox Cemetery, East Berlin:
Benjamin Wilcox Esq, died May 10, 1843 Aged 61. His wives– Betsey died Jan. 28 1831 Aged 45. Hepzibah Galpin died Aug. 10, 1853 Aged 57.

---

[8] Coffin, Margaret, *The History & Folklore of American Country Tinware 1700—1900*, p. 139.

certainly imply that the North sisters were decorators. There were eight sisters and only Olive married at a young age. Of the others, four were spinsters (Sarah, Beulah, Rachel and Marilla) and the rest married late in life—Julie at age 26, Lucy at age 32, and Patty at age 46. Lucy may have gone to paint for Albert since she was married in Steuben County, NY. Marilla North was also a cousin of Benjamin Wilcox. Her grandmother and Benjamin's father were sister and brother. Having relatives work for you in your business was a very common practice of the period. Not only did this practice help to keep the family united and interacting together, but it also kept any "trade secrets" within the confines of the family. At the time of Benjamin's letter in 1819, his cousin Marilla was 20 years old and unmarried. She would most likely have been available to spend the winter in Virginia flowering tinware.

It seems that Benjamin did not go to Virginia for many years. He was there in the winter of 1818/19, but from the winter of 1819/20 to 1822/23, the correspondence is from brother Richard in Petersburg to Benjamin in Middletown. Benjamin and Betsey had three children—Eliza [b. 1808], Samuel C. [b. 1811], and Edward [b. 1815]. Benjamin's wife died in 1831, and he remarried to his cousin Hepzibah Wilcox [1796—1853], widow of Norris Galpin. Hepzibah had been a decorator of tin before her first marriage. According to DeVoe: "A coffee-pot in the possession of the Galpin family is ornamented with gold leaf on black japan. The work was done at a Berlin tin-shop in 1818. An urn in the design has the initials H. W."[9] Hepzibah had a son by her first marriage, Henry Norris Galpin, who would in later years run the store that had originally belonged to the Pattison family.

Richard Wilcox [1780—1839], Benjamin's older brother and business partner, married first to Olive Porter [1783—1827] and they had four children. He married second to Betsey (Savage) Smith, and third to Laura (Savage) Smith. He ran the wintertime business in Petersburg, VA and he operated there from 1817 to 1823. His letters to Benjamin do not imply that he had decorators with him in Virginia, but only his workmen who made plain tinware on site. The japanned ware was sent to him from Connecticut. Excerpts from his letters tell about the progress of the business.

> *April 1819:* "I have sold all the Japan tin but four nest trunk & seven of sugar boxes the waiters have all been out some time and I have about three loads more of plain tin left...Mr. Holmes I think has made the best trip this time (of) any that has been made this winter in proportion to his load (it) amounted to about $80 & returned in $190 - $82 Spanish mills."

> *January 1820:* Richard has not received his order of tinplate from NYC. He has 6 or 8 peddlers waiting. He says Selden Peck and

---

[9] DeVoe, Shirley Spaulding, *The Tinsmiths of Connecticut* pp. 158-9.

Norris got their loads from Mr. Yale because Richard didn't arrive soon enough. "We have been verry much drove ever since we began but have a pretty good assortment on hand now, but it is a small one. Our workmen stick to pretty steady they do from thirty to thirty-three days work in a week, but they can not come up with your workmen at home."

November 1821: "I have got our tin plate and have got to work but am for the preasant verry much drove for tin ware, but intend to keep our heads out of water after a little time…I had to sell at seven pounds cash. I think I can sell all the tin that we can make at that price & they say they can get it at Mr. Yales shop for that price and I am determined not to lose any of my peddlers for not selling as low as they can get it there."

January 1822: "I should have wrote you sooner but I have been so drove in business that I have not had time to go up town for ten days past for on Friday I sent out five peddlers and on Saturday I had four more come in. Got them out on Wednesday they had been out but half hour and another come in & he was ready to go out, and they allmost wore me out…Inclosed you will find a draft for two hundred dollars which I expect will be as good as cash anywhere in Middletown and find it verry difficult to get United States money here at this time…I think it (a bank draft) is much the best way to convey money for the resque is considerable for I verry often here of late of the mails being robbed…Mr. Savage has not got back here yet, but I have heard from him since I wrote you last he wrote me from Norfolk and wrote that he was well but said that Bailey he thought was not doing much, and put a little to much whiskey in his water. And he wrote that Mr. Hendrix was in Hamton and had got to be a proper sott, he would get to much before breakfast and would lie on the counter all the rest of the day. I gave him power to settle our business with him and like wise with Mr. Bailey."

February 1822: "I wish you to give your opinion whether we had better come here another year or not for if we should I think we had better hire the place that we now occupy, for I think that I can hire it about as cheap for a year as I can for seven months and we have a plenty of sheds that we can store our waggons under and save the expense of shiping them home, if I cannot sell them, it would save us considerable in other property that would be better to have here than to ship it home."

April 1822: North Carolina money that his peddlers turn in is discounted at 5%. Richard says he is better off to purchase flour or other articles rather than exchange it.

November 1822: Richard goes to Virginia by way of NYC. "I have purchased 36 boxes of tinplate to send you, which Mssrs Phelps and Peck will ship to Middletown… I can only get 18 boxes out of the 100 boxes

Connecticut Courant June 23, 1800. (CSL).

I have purchased at this time to carry with me, the call is verry great for tin at this time. the tin he sends you will be $13 per box."

December 1822: "I want you should send on the Japan ware & other property at home as soon as posible if you have not shiped it…We have had a number of peddlers in before I got here. I have loaded three this week Mr. Darling is now in here his second time. He shiped on board the steam brigg at N York for Norfolk for twenty five dollars horse waggon & himself, which I think is the cheapest way any of our peddlers can get on…I would inform you I have got the same buildings I had last year at the same price & the same black girl for a cook."

January 1823: "Our peddlers are rather unfortunate this season. Mr Hubbard when he was in lost his pocketbook with $145 in it principle-ly tin money. he has never found it nor heard from it. he lost it not more than one hundred yards from our shop…Mr Pardy had his wag-gon broken open in Fredericksburg & two hundred twenty five prime muskratt taken from it. they were worth 37 cents per piece, supposed-ly was Baltimore peddlers that took them…Alfred Wilcox I here has lost his pocketbook with seven or eight dollars in it…Mr Richardson was taken up (arrested) in Fredericksburg for selling ware but got clear by telling them that his tin was manufactured in Petersburg & having his bill. This is a fair statement of our peddlers ill luck…North Carolina paper is today 7%…Times are hard and to use the Virginia phraise it's damed hard. it is such times as Virginia never saw before. there is a great many failures here and some pretty heavy ones within one week past & more expected every day. I have now concluded and have put my foot down that I will never come here no more to carry on business for Virginia is wore thread bare. she is poor as povity, more so this winter than ever owing to their crops being cut off the last summer by drought. I have thought and do think that by makeing a little differant arrangement in our business that we can make more money at home than we can here. that is to say move the shop up to my house & keep a small apartment of Yankee notions such as pins, needles, necklaces, thimbles & perhaps a few calico handkerchief, domestics, & C. If this should meet your approbation I would take care of the business and take the workmen, as you have enough to do on the farm and it would save your wife a heep of work."

February 1823: Tin is selling as well this winter as it ever had. "Our workmen stick to it tight. Jackson did week before last 14 days work. John did 12. Norris 8 1/2 and last week Norris did 9 days work. John Deming mashed one of his little fingers last week on Wednesday. he has done nothing since nor do I expect he will this week…I am quite sorry you shiped so much Japan tin for I can not sell it…The trunks & sugar boxes I had a plenty before the last ship-ment for we can scarsely give them away in this country."

March 11, 1823: "I shall probably be home by the 12th May as the Honorable State of Virginia has laid a tax on dry goods peddlers of $16 in every county & tin & pewter & other domestic peddlers of $10…to take effect the first day of May next."

March 22, 1823: I do not take but little money this season, as I wrote you before. I do not sell but little except plain tin ware & that you well know the sales will not amount to much, and then the discount on the money is so much that it takes nearly all the profitts off…I do not expect to make much this winter & if I have enough to pay off the workmen & the peddlers & pay for the tin plate & wire & a little to get home with, will be about as well as I expect…I shall ship home say 150 gross buttons that was left on here last season, some spoons, ivory combs, toothpicks, eyelett needles, Japan ware, a few of Freedom Hart's combs, & I shall make clean work when I break up."

April 1823: The workmen have arrived back home in Connecticut. "I am now here alone. nothing to do. I have broken up house keeping…I am now only waiting for H Bowers, P Smith, Lewis & Darling to come in & I shall then be ready to start for home & leave this cursed place."

It seems that 1823 was the last year that R. & B. Wilcox operated in Virginia. After that time they continued business in Connecticut, although it is not known for how long a period. As Benjamin was engaging himself in the cotton mill business with Shubael Pattison at this time, perhaps Richard did most of the tinning business as he had suggested in his January 1823 letter.

Sylvester Wilcox [1788—1854], another brother to Benjamin, was also a tinner. He married Lurania Dickenson [b. 1892] and settled in Rome, NY. There are also correspondences between him and Benjamin that relate to the business of R. & B. Wilcox.

June 1818: "I wish you to sen one good workman to work by the month or by the days work for I am in great want of one as soon as possible for I am a going to commence my business in Utica next week…I think that my business will bee much better their then it is in Rome."

July 1818: "I did not think that jurnaman wages were so high their as you rite for I think that I cannot give more that 20$ per month & pair their exspences up heir. If you will send on your apprentis Daniel Stockin I will give you for him 20$ per month for one year…If you can send me one hundred dollars worth of Jappan tin & give me creddet for the same untill I can disspose of the same I shall be vary glad if you would."

May 1820: "As for the southerd expedishon I shold be vary glad to go on for you this fall if you wold give mee such wages as it wold answer my purpos. But as for going for $25 per month I cannot go for that. But if you will alow me $30 per month & will let me bring my apprentis with mee I will com down & go to work for you for six or 7 month & you may alout mee for my boy just what you think he earns you."

In 1822 Sylvester had apprentices working for him and he sent out at least three peddlers. He still ordered japan ware from Benjamin, and this may mean that Sylvester did not do any decorating in his shop. He also had a tinshop in Palmyra, NY at the time, and Josiah Dickenson, a former apprentice, was running that shop while Sylvester stayed in Rome. In 1824 he asked Benjamin for tools and for more japan ware. In 1826 he said he could not afford to pay a journeyman. In 1830 he was not doing much business and did not have the money to buy stock, so he concentrated on collecting debts. His own mortgage payment was coming due and he wrote to Benjamin saying: "Sir if that I cannot git along & pay that amount I shal have to com down & sea you & Richard & you will have to help me to the monney." By 1831 things had improved and Sylvester ordered a full set of Seth Peck's tinware machines.

Daniel Wilcox [b. 1785] was the last brother and he resided in Deerfield, NY. He apparently was not a tinner as were the other brothers, although he did occasionally assist Benjamin in collecting outstanding debts owed to the firm of R. & B. Wilcox. In one of Sylvester's letters dated May 1820, he says that Daniel asks if Benjamin can get him a job on the big canal for $26 to $30 a month. This was most likely the Farmington Canal, which was in the initial planning stages in 1820, with actual ground breaking in 1825 and completion in 1828.

John Deming

John Deming [1769—1800] was a Berlin tinner who married Roxy Galpin [1769—1844]. His son Horace [1788—1845] was also a tinner and was working for Augustus Filley in the Lansingburg, NY shop in 1816. John Jr. [b. 1799] was probably the John Deming who worked for R. & B. Wilcox in Petersburg VA. His daughter Roxy [b. 1796] may have been a decorator (see Fig. 1.1). She married Col. William Buckley [1797—1878], a tinner who manufactured tinner's tools at his Berlin Street shop. Roxy apparently died young as Col. Buckley remarried in 1827. Lardner Deming was John's brother, and a Berlin merchant who sold tinware as well as general merchandise.

John Dunham

John Dunham was probably the son of Solomon [b. 1732], and a Berlin tinner who signed the 1813 price agreement. The shop where he did tinning and japanning was on his property near Elijah Loveland's tavern and Col. Buckley's place. He bought tinplate from Pattison & Peck, and also sold japanned tin to them, as well as to John Hubbard. His father Solomon was a tinner by trade and is said to have trained his son-in-law

300 Boxes Tin Plate, and Wire, for fale for Cafh or 60 or 365 days credit, by JOHN and C. DEMING. Cafh paid for heavy Pork in the Hog. Farmington, 1 November.

Connecticut Courant Nov. 1, 1798. (CSL).

Abel Porter. Lardner Deming, the Berlin merchant, was another son-in-law of Solomon's.

John Hubbard

John Hubbard was probably the son of Abijah Hubbard and Achsah Beckley, born 1768 and died 1845. His wife was Catharine King. The account books kept by John in his tin business for the years of 1818 to 1822 are preserved at the Connecticut Historical Society (see Appendix E). The books indicate that he had a lucrative business in plain and japanned ware. He also trained apprentices and sent out peddlers. He had two daughters who are known to have painted for him (one was Mary). A son John [b. 1809] was also a tinner. John Hubbard's account books list that he would sometimes purchase plain or decorated wares from John Dunham and Lysis Lamb.

RUN away from the subscriber, on the night of the 19th inst. two BOYS, who were serving as apprentices, in the Tinners Trade. Said Boys are about 19 years of age, and one of them whose name is *Elijah Howard* is about five feet ten inches high, with short brown hair and light eyes, he carried off with him several Coats, one of blue Broadcloth, several pair of Partaloons, one pair of them white another of black Velvet and another of striped Cotton, a Vest of the same striped Cotton. All persons are forbid harboring or employing said Howard, as I shall exact payment for his services. All persons are forbid trusting him, as I shall pay no debt of his contracting. JOHN HUBBARD. Berlin, Oct. 29. 79

Connecticut Courant Oct. 29, 1806 (CSL).

Lamb Family

James Lamb [1777—1833] was a Berlin tinner who had received his training from Shubael Pattison. He married first to Huldah Treat [1779—1811] and had sons Lysis [1801—1862] and Lewis. A second marriage to Chloe Beckley [1782—1862] produced two daughters and four more sons. James' son Lysis and his son-in-law James B. Carpenter were active with him in the business, and the firm was known as Lamb & Carpenter. His youngest son Lorenzo [1826—1909] and Linus Porter, a brother-in-law of Lysis, also worked with them in the company.

The Lamb family business was a very successful operation, and they sent out peddlers to traverse the country side. In *Recollections of Berlin*, Jane Dodd told of the hours that she and James' niece, Fidelia Porter, spent in his rag room looking for calico pieces for their rag dolls. James Lamb had invented a cooking stove that was the first of its kind. It was of a square upright style adorned with brass urns in the corners. The fire was built in the area above the oven, and allowed the heat to circulate around the oven.[10]

Jesse Eddy

The shop of Jesse Eddy [1785—1840] was on the Main Street in Berlin. Jane Dodd in recalling her childhood memories says : "While thinking of the attractions of the tin shops, I must not forget the great fascination of the long room in Mr. Eddy's shop where the painting was most artistically done on teapots, cake boxes and various household utensils. It was my great delight to be allowed to stand behind those young women who did the work and watch their every movement."[11]

John Goodrich Sr.

Another signer of the 1813 agreement, John Goodrich Sr. [1734—1816]

---

[10] Brandegee, Emily S., *Historical Papers—Berlin Connecticut*, p. 42.
[11] Meyers, Doris Vroom, *Berlin: Other Times, Other Voices*, p. 50

was a Berlin tinner and many of his descendants worked in the business as well. John Sr. worked with John Dunham in a shop near the center of town. John Jr. [1776—1858] was a tinner and still listed as such in 1850 when he was 74 years old. He worked with his son Darius [1799—1867]. John Sr.'s daughter Rebecca was married to tinner Lemuel North.

Samuel Kelsey

Samuel Kelsey [1777—1816] was a tinner of Berlin who signed the 1813 price agreement. His daughter Miranda was married to Alfred Wilcox, who was mentioned in the Wilcox letters and also was employed by the J & E North Company. His other daughter Almira was married first to Richard Wilcox's son Willis, and secondly to Edmund North, owner of J & E North Co. (as his third wife).

Patrick Clark

Patrick Clark was a Meriden tinsmith who had a shop on East Main Street. He had been associated with Shubael Pattison in 1801 when that firm was known as Pattison, Porter & Co. His sons Patrick, Jr. and Samuel worked in the tin business with him. In the mid 1800s their firm became Stedman & Clark, at which time Patrick, Jr. built a new shop.

Patrick Clark had been a signer of the 1813 price agreement and tin lamps were among the various tinware items that he produced. Richard Wilcox wrote to his brother Benjamin in February 1823: "The lamps they will not sell, for the country people use light wood alltogether for candles in this country. & it appears to me that Mr Clark shaved you pretty well in the price of them, for when I came on last fall Mr Clark's son came on with me as far as N York to sell lamps. I do not recollect exactly what he asked for them but it appears to me that it was not over about one half you gave for them…I have seen men from the eastward where peddlers traveled last summer from Meriden that told me that they were sold for 6 cents apiece by them. And I presume they would not sell without some little profit."

Yale Family

Five brothers in Meriden, Connecticut were all engaged in the tinware business. They were the sons of Samuel Yale, the first manufacturer in that town. In 1791 he had begun to make cut nails which were all "headed" by hand. In 1794 he also started making pewter buttons. Samuel and his sons added tinware production to the enterprise carried on at their shop near the corner of East Main and Broad Streets. The father died in 1810, and William [1784—1833], Samuel Jr. [b. 1787], and Ivah [b. 1792] continued the business making japanned tin and lamp trimmings. The other two brothers, Charles [1790—1834] and Selden [1795—1823], carried on the family business in Richmond, Virginia, dealing in tinware and Brittannia ware. The Yales sent out peddlers from both the Connecticut and Virginia operations. Richard Wilcox, in his November 1821 letter to his brother, suggests a rivalry between his firm and the Yales.

WANTED one or two Journeymen Tinners, to whom punctual payment will be made every three boxes of tin. Also one or two likely boys 15 or 16 years of age, as apprentices to the tin trade, where they can be well instructed. Enquire of ENOCH KELSY.
Berlin, Nov. 11, 1799

Connecticut Courant Nov. 11, 1799 (CSL).

Berlin and East Berlin, Connecticut (circa 1820)

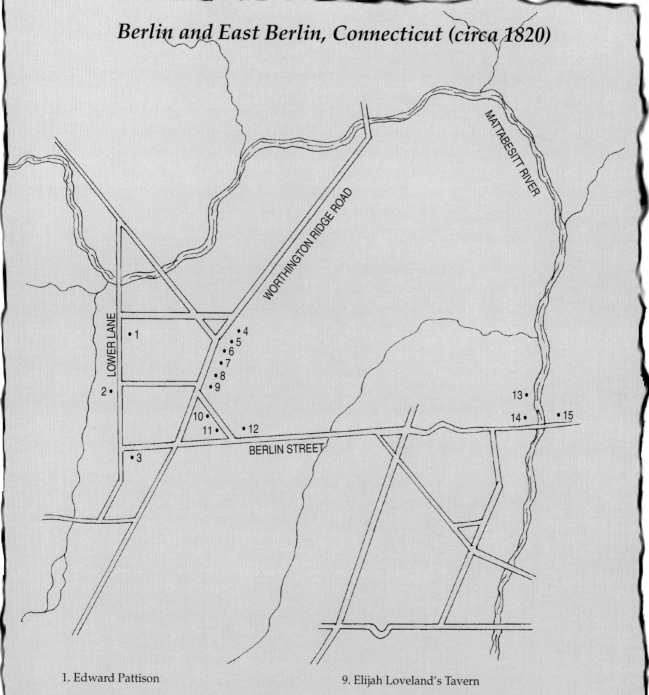

1. Edward Pattison

2. Shubail Patttison's shop moved here in 1830

3. John Hubbard

4. James Lamb

5. Blakesley Barnes

6. Hiram Mygatt

7. Jesse Eddy

8. Shubael Pattison's store & tinshop

9. Elijah Loveland's Tavern

10. John Dunham and John Goodrich, Sr.

11. John Buckman

12. Col. William Buckley's tinmen's tools shop

13. Cotton mill of Pattison & Wilcox. Later Roys & Wilcox made tinner' tools. Then it became Peck, Stow & Wilcox.

14. R. & B. & Wilcox.

15. J & E. North tinmen's tools shop

BERLIN CT: Introduction to the Photographs

The origin of tinware manufacture in America took place 250 years ago. The tinware produced prior to the Revolutionary War was sold as plain tin. The English art of japanned and flowered tinware became the preferred product when tinplate work resumed after the war. Decorated tin is rarely signed. When a painted signature is discovered, it is generally assumed to be the original decorator who signed it while the brush was still in hand. Signatures that are scratched into the background paint may have been done by the decorator, or may have been done by an owner of the piece. Researching this name, along with towns, dates, or any other information present, may prove fruitful in determining if a scratched signature is actually that of the decorator.

Most of the tinsmiths of the late 18th and early 19th centuries learned the trade in the Berlin area, either directly from the Pattison family, or from smiths who had originally trained with the Pattisons. Eventually many of these newly trained smiths left Connecticut with the migrations to New York and the Ohio area. Many times it is possible to identify a painted characteristic that shows evidence of someone who had received his or her initial training back in Berlin even though the particular piece has a provenance outside of Connecticut. This is interesting historically in helping to understand how this successful business spread throughout the countryside, but unfortunately it does not give us names of specific decorators or even the tinshop of manufacture.

It is necessary to keep in mind when studying Chapter One that these pieces represent the entire Berlin area, and not the work of any specific tinshop. Though similar characteristics seem apparent, the pieces may represent the work of several shops, and there could be several explanations for this. The design or motif was learned at one shop and continued at another shop, possibly after an apprenticeship had been completed. A journeyman painter, accustomed to his or her own designs, worked for more than one tinshop. It must also be considered that many decorators were young girls. Those who became proficient at the craft would certainly begin to design their own motifs and arrangements. They may have exchanged ideas with friends who were employed in other shops. Competition in regard to designs was not of particular concern in this period of our history. The major competition between the shops was to produce the products, and to get the peddlers' wagons loaded and on the road.

The decorated pieces from Berlin have been divided into four major groups, with two of these further subdivided. There were a great many tinsmiths operating in this area (see Appendix F), and it is likely that many other types of designs rightfully belong here. Without identifiable signatures or family attributions, we are unable to include more in the Berlin section; however, many will be addressed in the Miscellaneous Section of a future volume.

Figure captions by Lois Tucker

GROUP I

A small covered canister with the scratched signature Roxy Deming Berlin (Fig. 1.1) begins this group. Roxy was the daughter of John Deming, and more information about her can be found in the Chapter text. In order to help simplify the designation of painted characteristics for this group, it has been subdivided into three sections– A, B, and C.

SECTION A

Fig. 1.1. Covered canister 3 ⅝" (9.20 cm). Black. The small canister has painted on each side an elongated flower with alizarin and white overstrokes. Yellow crosshatching is positioned between the flowers, and three green pointed leaves with yellow veining are above and below the center. A yellow ribbon with red dots is painted around the rim of the cover. Although this piece shows much wear, it is important for this study because of the scratched inscription on the bottom. *When this you see, remember me. Roxy Deming. Berlin.*
Private Collection

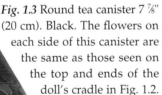

Fig. 1.2. Tin Cradle 8 ½" (21.6 cm). Red. The design on the sides of this doll's cradle is identical to the preceding example. The flowers are painted in light salmony-pink with alizarin and white overtones. The crosshatching and the small strokes along the stem lines are alizarin. Painted on the two ends and the top of the hood is a similar design except that the flowers are heart-shaped.

Courtesy, Connecticut Historical Society, Hartford, CT

Fig. 1.3 Round tea canister 7 ⅞" (20 cm). Black. The flowers on each side of this canister are the same as those seen on the top and ends of the doll's cradle in Fig. 1.2. A row of yellow brushstrokes is painted around the shoulder of the canister.

Private Collection

Fig. 1.4. Oval tea canister 4 ¾" (12.1 cm). Black. The two large flowers on this canister are a variation of those seen in Figs. 1.1 and 1.2. The alizarin and white overstrokes flow upward from the stem area in the lower section of the blossoms, and then are painted crosswise in the upper section. Yellow and green leaflets are seen as well as two groups of three buds. An alizarin overtone is painted across one-half of each bud.

Anonymous

Fig. 1.5. Coffee Pot 9" tall (22.9 cm). Black. This coffee pot demonstrates a variation of what we've seen thus far. The two flowers are now in a vertical alignment, and the leaves are rounded at their tips. The leaflets at the head of the flowers are green on one side and yellow on the other. Note the two curliques among the stems.

Anonymous

SECTION B

Fig. 1.6. Tea canister 4 ¾" (12.1 cm). Black. Four round motifs with green and yellow leaflet groups adorn this canister. The overtones on two of the red motifs are painted crosswise, while the other two have alizarin painted completely across one-half of the unit as seen in Fig. 1.4. Groups of yellow dots and hash lines across the base of the leaflets are also seen. A yellow rick rack stroke is used on the shoulder and around the base edge.

Anonymous

Fig. 1.7. Teapot 4 ¾" (12.1 cm). Black. The main flower on this teapot now shows added petals on each side of the central round head. Buds have alizarin over half their area with a white line along the inner edge. Large rounded leaves are again seen, as are yellow curliques.

Anonymous

Fig. 1.8. Coffee Pot 9" tall (22.9 cm). Black. The design on each side of this coffee pot shows a group of four red motifs with yellow crosshatching in the center. The narrow alizarin and white overtones are positioned crosswise on two units, while the other two have a fan-like arrangement with an undulating "cobra" stroke at the head. Green leaflets are accented with yellow.

Collection of Patricia Hatch

Fig. 1.9. Bread Basket 10 ⅞" (27.6 cm). Black. This octagonal bread basket has a central unit with narrow overtones painted crosswise. The four smaller buds are painted as those in Figs. 1.6, 1.7, and 1.8. Juxtaposed green and yellow leaflets complete the design. Note the yellow brushstroke border.

Collection of Mona D. Rowell

Fig. 1.10. Trunk 9 ⅞" (25.1 cm). Black. The swagged design on the front of this trunk shows a central unit with narrow alizarin and white overtones, and three buds below. Two groups of four buds are similar to Fig. 1.8, including the "cobra" stroke. Red stems connect the buds to the main unit, and olive green leaflets have yellow accents. The name *Submit Fletcher* painted on the lower front most likely indicates the owner rather than the decorator. The trunk end shows a group of four buds as displayed on the front, but the leaflets are arranged differently. Yellow ribbons surround the trunk end and three sides of the front. The lid has a blue ribbon around the outer edge with groups of red strokes in the four corners.

Collection of Jane Domenico

SECTION C

Fig. 1.11. Trunk 8 ⅞" (22.5 cm). Black. A swagged design across this trunk depicts a central motif that has a scalloped outer edge. Narrow alizarin and white overtones alternating with groups of white dots are painted within the scallops. A pinwheel arrangement is used in the center. Two small buds are positioned to each side of the center unit, and they show the same overtones as Figs. 1.8 and 1.10. Opposing groups of yellow and green leaflets connect the motifs, and there is crosshatching in between. The ends of this trunk, as well as the lid decoration, are nearly identical to those on Fig. 1.10.

Collection of Harriet Syversen

Fig. 1.12. Trunk 9 ¼" (23.5 cm). Black. This design is similar to the preceding example. The scalloped flower shows two curved brushstroke groups—one in alizarin and one in white. An alizarin ribbon runs across the center along with white dots. The four small buds have been previously seen. Green and yellow leaflets, painted in semi-impasto technique, join the buds to the main flower. A row of graceful green brushstrokes surrounds the edge of the lid, and groups of yellow strokes enhance the corners and handle. A yellow ribbon on the trunk ends to form an X.

Collection of Jeanne Gearin

Fig. 1.13. Trunk 9 ¼" (23.5 cm). Black. Swagged across the front of this trunk is a string of round flowers separated by green leaflets accented with yellow. The units show the same overtone treatment and "cobra" strokes as in the two previous examples, but they are here painted in white and blue. Note the yellow curliques.

Collection of Estelle Hall

Fig. 1.14. Trunk 9 ¾" (24.8 cm). Black. A swag design with a scalloped central flower and four buds that are executed with blue paint. Overpainting on each of these units is a swirled stroke painted by a wet-technique in which two colors (red and white) are used on the brush. Yellow and green semi-impasto leaflets are placed between the flowers, with yellow hash lines also seen. The lid shows a red stripe and yellow brushstrokes.

Private Collection

CHARACTERISTICS OF BERLIN AREA DECORATION

The line drawings following each section will demonstrate in greater detail than the preceding photographs the major design characteristics of the tinware attributed to the Berlin area tinshops.

Groups I and III are subdivided to help separate the whole groups' characteristics which are similar yet have distinctions of their own. These distinctions verify the assumptions stated previously in this chapter that the designs may represent the work of more than one Berlin tinshop.

Groups III and IV contain many examples of trunks with painted bands. These have been illustrated by drawing only the left side of the trunk face. The design for the right side is a repeat of that on the left, with occasional examples showing the right side to be a mirror image.

Colors found on Berlin area pieces:
> Red—vermilion, salmony pink
> Green—medium, dark, or olive
> Yellow—light, medium, dark, or ochre
> White for overtones—transparent or opaque
> White for bands—opaque
> Alizarin for overtones—usually dark
> Blue—medium blue for bands or border strokes (not a commonly found color)
> Black—occasionally used

Types of decorated tinware found:
Every piece of tinware that is known to have been japanned was produced by the Berlin area tinshops.
> See Appendix B for a complete listing of these various items.

Note that large trunks in Groups I and III which measure approximately 8 or 9″ in width often are narrower from front to back when compared to trunks of similar size from other tin areas. This gives the trunks the appearance of being taller than would be expected for their size, although their height is comparable to that of other shops.

Illustration selections and line drawings by Lois Tucker

Group I—Section A

A1. Background: Black (one example known in red).

A2. Designs: Geometrically balanced.

A3. Flowers:

> a. Lobular blossom in red with alizarin and white overtones painted crosswise at the head end.

Refer to page xv for the guide to interpretation of the line drawings.

b. Heart-shaped flowers, sometimes with added petals at the base end. Overtones may be painted crosswise at the head end.

c. Rose buds.

d. Small oval buds with alizarin stroke over half their area. A white line will edge the alizarin within the bud.

e. Stems are red.

A4. Leaves:
    a. Pointed or round forms.
    b. Veining in yellow. Side veins may be curved or straight, and occasionally extend beyond the leaf edges.
    c. Yellow squiggles may sprout from the stems.

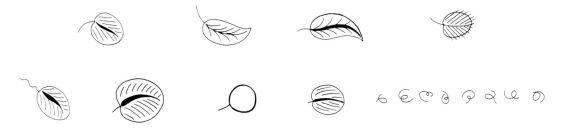

A5. Borders: Ribbon stroke, rope stroke or brushstroke groups. Trunk ends may have a diagonal border arrangement.

A6. Striping: Seldom found.

Group I—Section B

B1. Background: Black

B2. Designs: Geometrically balanced

B3. Flowers:

    a. <u>Round red units arranged as a group of four with yellow crosshatching in the center of the group</u> or a single large red unit.

    b. <u>Alizarin and white crescent-shaped overtones painted crosswise</u> as in A3a. Overtones may also be painted as brushstroke groupings.

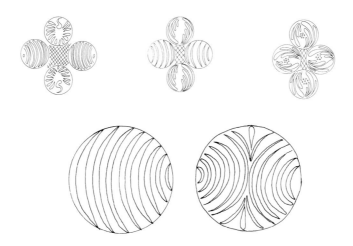

    c. <u>Alizarin or white undulating "cobra" stroke.</u>

    d. Small round buds with alizarin painted across half as under A3d.

    e. Petaled flowers with crosshatching in center opening.

    f. Yellow squiggles nested among flowers. Formed by one loop and a long wavy line that diminishes in width to its end.

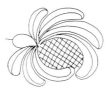

    g. Stems are red.

B4. Leaves:

    a. Leaflets in green and yellow groups.

    b. Green leaflets may have yellow accents.

    c. Large oval leaves with yellow veining.

B5. Trunk Lids, Ends and Borders:

    a. Trunks have ribbon painted along each edge of the front, ends, and top, usually in yellow.

    b. <u>Ribbon stroke on edge of trunk lid may be blue.</u>

    c. <u>Trunk ends have four round bud units with yellow and green leaflets.</u>

B6. Striping: Seldom found.

Group I—Section C

C1. Background: Black

C2. Designs: Geometrically balanced.

C3. Painting Technique: Semi-impasto painting sometimes found (yellow, green, and white pigments).

C4. Flowers:

    a. Scalloped flowers (usually red) used as the central motif.

    b. Overtones in alizarin and white, occasionally with green and yellow also.

    c. Interesting arrangements formed within the flower by the overtones—pinwheels, crosshatching, large swag or ribbon stroke across flower, or brushstroke groups.

    d. Round red buds with crosswise overtones and <u>"cobra stroke"</u> as described in B3c.

    e. Yellow squiggle stroke as in B3f.

    f. Rose buds occasionally found.

C5. Leaves:

    a. Green and yellow leaflets.

    b. Oval and pointed leaves with yellow veining.

C6. Trunk Fronts: Edged on all sides with ribbon stroke.

C7. Trunk Lids:

    a. Lids edged with yellow ribbon stroke, occasionally green.

    b. Rope stroke in yellow or red.

    c. Yellow "lattice fence" stroke.

C8. Trunk Ends:

    a. Ribbon stroke forming an X.

    b. <u>Four round bud units</u> as described under B5c occasionally found.

C9. Striping: Seldom found.

Typical Group I-C Designs

GROUP II

The 2-sheet waiter (Fig. 1.15) that begins this group has been attributed to Berlin manufacture by its owners.

Fig. 1.15. 2-sheet waiter 17¼" (43.5 cm). Black. A red circle with alizarin overpainting is the central motif of this geometrically balanced design. Eight groups of red and green circles, red scallops, rose buds and leaflets surround it. Very slender green and yellow strokes are used for the leaflets as well as the strokes along the flange of the waiter. A tight yellow rick rack rims the floor near the crease. Notice the frilly tendrils on each side of the rose buds. This piece has some restoration.

Collection of Muriel Baker (deceased)

Fig. 1.16. 2-sheet waiter 17½" (44.3 cm). Black. Another geometrically balanced design with red units displaying alizarin and white overtones. Red scallops surround a central diamond-shaped unit with yellow crosshatching used in the openings. Leaflet groups similar to those in Fig. 1.15 now show a narrow yellow edging along each olive green stroke. Green leaflets edged with yellow were also seen in Figs. 1.8 and 1.10. Large leaves with yellow veins are used, and narrow yellow rick rack forms the borders. Four elongated rose buds extend from the junctions of the scallops. Red stems attach the roses and large leaves.

Courtesy, The American Museum, Bath, England

Fig. 1.17. 2-sheet waiter 17¾" (45.1 cm). Black. This waiter, although in poor condition, shows a large round central motif similar to Fig. 1.15. Four round buds and two flowers formed by red circles are joined to the main unit by red stems. Leaflet groups of yellow- edged green and yellow strokes are again seen, and now have a yellow dot at their focal point. The green bud at the center top has tendrils extending from it. The painted overtones are too worn to discern. Borders of yellow rick rack are painted as on Fig. 1.16.

Collection of Ruth Carter

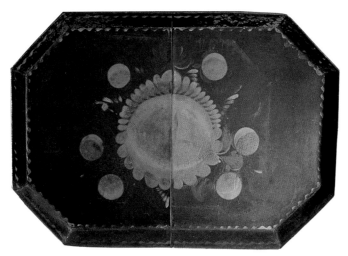

Fig. 1.18. 2-sheet waiter 17" (43.2 cm). Black. This waiter also shows signs of wear but illustrates a large central flower unit that resembles a rose, with petals painted around its edge. A large alizarin oval in the center of this rose also has smaller strokes around its edge. Another dark alizarin stroke can be seen painted across the lower half of the uppermost petals. The six buds show the alizarin strokes as well, but the white overtones have been worn off. The green bud at the center top, as well as the leaflets, have been seen in previous examples.

Private Collection

Fig. 1.19. Molasses Cup 4⅛" (10.2 cm) Black. The rose on this piece has the same treatment as that in Fig. 1.18. Small buds are attached by red stems. The leaflet groups again show the yellow dot in the base.

State Museum of Pennsylvania, Harrisburg, PA

Group II

1. Background: Black

2. Designs: Geometrically balanced.

3. Flowers:

    a. Stylized roses and buds with alizarin and white overtones.

    b. Roses may have petals extending across the top of the blossom. These petals will have a stroke of alizarin painted as one stroke across their lower ends.

    c. Round buds which have alizarin painted over ½ to ¾ of their area.

    d. Flower stems, if present, are red.

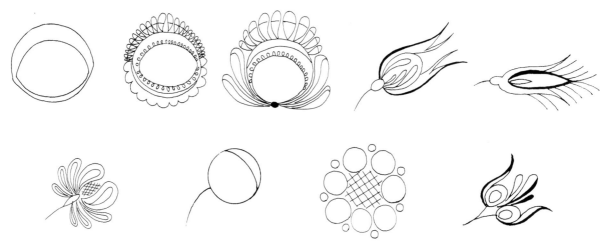

4. Leaves:

    a. Single stroke leaflet groups painted all green or half green and half yellow.

    b. Green leaflets often have yellow outline on one side.

    c. Large round leaves.

    d. Yellow center vein on larger leaf forms.

5. Borders:

    a. Yellow ribbon stroke (tiny and very compact).

    b. Yellow single brushstroke (very narrow) painted in alternating direction.

6. Striping: Rarely found.

GROUP III

The beginning item for this group (Fig. 1.20) is another piece with a Berlin history, and is still in the possession of a Berlin resident. This group is also subdivided into three sections–A, B, and C.

SECTION A

Fig. 1.20a and 1.20b. Trunk 9" (22.9 cm). Asphaltum. The painted red band is adorned with alternating chevron groupings of alizarin and white overtones. Red swags swoop under the band, and there are yellow brushstroke groups nesting within the openings formed by the swags. Yellow groups also hang downward at the swag junctures. The trunk end shows a round motif with alizarin and white painted across it, along with yellow crosshatching. White and yellow leaflet groups surround this motif. Note that there is no green color used on this piece of tinware. The lid has an outer border of yellow rope strokes, and an inner border of red ribbon. Notice also that there is no border design painted on the front face of the lid, nor on the upper edge of the trunk end.

Collection of Katrina Bowers Shepard (deceased)

Fig. 1.21. Dome-topped canister 5" height (12.7 cm). Black. This piece has a red swag decoration similar to Fig. 1.20. Red and yellow in combination are used on the top lid. No border is found on the edge of the lid, and again no green color is used.

Collection of Phyllis Sherman

Fig. 1.22a and 1.22b. Trunk 8 ¾" (22.2 cm). Asphaltum.. The red band along the trunk front has alternating alizarin and white overtones resembling "candy striping". The swags below the band are similar to Fig. 1.20. The lid has a yellow ribbon stroke and stripe around the edge with brushstroke groupings in the corners. The trunk ends show red rope diagonals with four groupings in yellow. There are no borders on the lid face, and no green colors are used.

Collection of Liz Bach

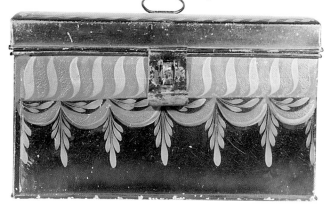

Fig. 1.23a and 1.23b. Trunk 8 ¾" (22.2 cm). Asphaltum. This red band with the "candy striping" has two swags below. The swags have an alizarin ribbon overtone with two white dots placed at the narrow sections of that ribbon. A yellow brushstroke group fills that space formed by the swag, and there is a yellow ribbon along the swag's lower edge. The lid has groupings of three white berries with extended yellow strokes. The trunk's end design is a variation on Fig. 1.22. Again there is no green used and no borders painted on the facing edge of the lid.

HSEAD Collection at The Museum of American Folk Art, New York, NY

Fig. 1.24a and 1.24b. Trunk 9½" (24.1 cm). Asphaltum. The front of this trunk (only the left half is pictured) has a red band and two swags as did the previous example. The overpainting on the bands consists of horizontally positioned strokes in alizarin and white. Yellow dots and crosshatching are also used. A dark green swag is painted along the lower edge of the red swag, and this is in turn edged with a yellow ribbon. The end unit shows a similarity to Fig. 1.20 but now has the surrounding curved leaflets painted in yellow and green. A border of yellow ribbon is used on the front face of the lid and on the ends.

Collection of Eleanor Pattison

Fig. 1.25a and 1.25b. Trunk 8⅞" (22.5 cm). Asphaltum. The alizarin overtone on the red swag is painted as a ribbon stroke with two yellow dots. The end unit is similar to Fig. 1.24 except for the overpainting on the red motif which has a group of alizarin strokes on the right side and white on the left. Yellow crosshatching is also used. The decoration on the lid now has brush strokes added around the handle.

Collection of Kenneth and Paulette Tuttle

Fig. 1.26. Trunk 9 ¼" (23.5 cm). Asphaltum. Red swags are positioned on the front and each end of this trunk. The swags have a large alizarin ribbon with yellow dots. Again no green is used, and there are no borders on the lid faces.

Private Collection

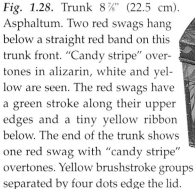

Fig. 1.28. Trunk 8 ⅞" (22.5 cm). Asphaltum. Two red swags hang below a straight red band on this trunk front. "Candy stripe" overtones in alizarin, white and yellow are seen. The red swags have a green stroke along their upper edges and a tiny yellow ribbon below. The end of the trunk shows one red swag with "candy stripe" overtones. Yellow brushstroke groups separated by four dots edge the lid.

Courtesy, Winterthur Museum, Winterthur, DE

Fig. 1.27. Molasses Cup 4" height (10.1 cm). Asphaltum. A swagged red band with alizarin and white overtones adorns this small piece.

Collection of Robert Roché

Fig. 1.29. Trunk 8" (20.3 cm). Asphaltum. Two red swags overpainted with alizarin, white and yellow adorn the front of this trunk, and a single swag is on each end. Groups of yellow brushstrokes as seen in Fig. 1.25a nest above the swags. Crosshatching at the end of the longest stroke has been seen in Fig. 1.26. Two yellow groups flow down below the hasp. The lid has yellow ribbon painted from corner to corner, and two opposing yellow groups run between the handle posts. Red dots and two red brushstroke groups are also seen.

Courtesy, Winterthur Museum, Winterthur, DE

Fig. 1.30. Trunk 8 ¼" (21 cm). Asphaltum. This trunk has a total of eight red swags with alizarin, white and yellow overtones as seen in Fig. 1.29. Above each red swag is a dark green stroke topped by a group of yellow brushstrokes. More yellow groups hang down like tassels between the swags. A green ribbon with yellow dots is painted along the lid face. The decoration on the lid is similar to those already seen.

Collection of Maryjane Clark

Fig. 1.31. Trunk 9 ⅛" (23.2 cm). Asphaltum. A straight red band as well as two small swags on each side of a larger scalloped swag grace this trunk front. Overtone treatment has been seen previously. Each end shows a floral spray with three large blossoms. Two large serrated leaves are positioned on the lower stem, but the dark green color makes them difficult to see. The lid is bordered by a red band overpainted with a black rope stroke, while yellow brushstroke groupings finish the lid decoration.

Courtesy, Abby Aldrich Rockefeller Folk Art Center Williamsburg, VA

SECTION B

Fig. 1.32. Trunk 8 ⅞" (22.5 cm) Black. A red scalloped band is seen on the front of this trunk. The overtone "candy striping" strokes on the band are executed in alternating white, alizarin, and blue. Ribbon strokes are used as a border design and are blue on the lid and yellow elsewhere. Red brushstroke groups are found in the lid corners and at the handle. The decoration on the trunk ends shows the same design as the front but with two scallops rather than the four.

Collection of Harriet Syversen

Fig. 1.33. Trunk 10" (25.4 cm) Black. Red swags with a scalloped lower edge adorn this piece, with two swags on the front and one on each end. The overtone painting is alizarin, white, and blue "candy striping". A burst of yellow strokes fills the opening formed by the swag. The lid and border design is the same as Fig. 1.32.

Collection of Marianne Hauck

Fig. 1.34. Trunk End 5" (12.7 cm) Asphaltum. The asphaltum background is severely worn on this piece, but the design clearly shows the swagged blue band which is overpainted with red and white brushstroke groups. The trunk front shows two of these blue swags. The lid design and border strokes are similar to Figs. 1.32 and 1.33 although painted in yellow.

Collection of Ida Fraioli

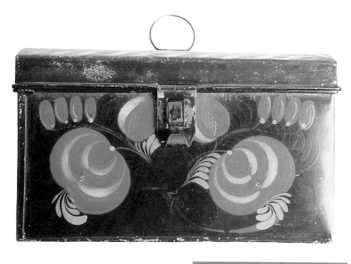

SECTION C

Fig. 1.35a and 1.35b. Trunk 8⅞" (22.5 cm). Asphaltum. A floral spray is used on the front of this trunk. The large red flowers and the buds have alizarin and white overtones, and are attached to red stems. Three large leaves of semitransparent dark green are positioned in the center. The end units are similar to Fig. 1.25b, but here the leaflets are not curved. Decoration on the lid is a variant of Fig. 1.20. No border is used on the lid facing edges.

Collection of Lois Tucker

Fig. 1.36. Trunk. 10" (25.4 cm). Asphaltum. The similarity with the previous example is evident. The alizarin and white overtones are painted in nearly vertical bands across the motifs. The end unit is similar to that on Fig. 1.23. Green leaves on the front and the two green groups on the end are difficult to discern in this black and white photograph.

Private Collection

Fig. 1.37. Mug 4⅞" height (12.4 cm). Asphaltum. This mug illustrates the same overtone treatment as seen in Fig. 1.36. The dark red units are surrounded by yellow and green leaflets as previously seen.

Courtesy, The American Museum, Bath, England

Fig. 1.38. Tea Canister 5" (12.7 cm). Asphaltum. A similar design to the previous example although the painting appears less skillfully executed.

HSEAD Collection at The Museum of American Folk Art, New York, NY

Group III—Section A

A1. Background: Asphaltum or black.

A2. Designs: Geometrically balanced. <u>Green color seldom used</u>.

A3. Red Painted Bands:
   a. Bands are straight and/or swagged. Swags may be scalloped on lower edge. Green swag
      occasionally painted along either side of the red swag.
   b. Overtones on bands—
         1.) Alternating chevron brushstroke groupings in alizarin and white.
         2.) Alizarin brushstroke groups with white dots.

         3.) Alizarin and white swags on the red swags.

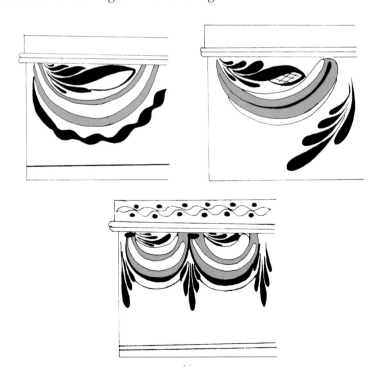

4.) Alternating alizarin and white single strokes in "candy stripe" arrangement.

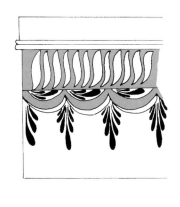 

5.) Ribbon stroke in alizarin with white or yellow dots.

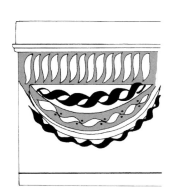 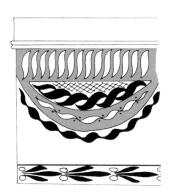 

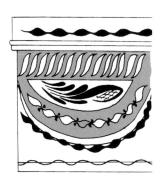 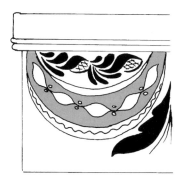

A4. Lid Facing Edge (front and end) Borders:

a. No decoration is the usual.

b. If decoration is present, a yellow ribbon is most common.

c. Large green ribbon stroke with yellow dots.

d. End face may have different border from the front face.

A5. Trunk Ends:

a. <u>Single round red flower form surrounded by four leaflet groups (either curved or straight strokes) in yellow and white or yellow and green.</u> Overtones in alizarin and white usually painted crosswise. They may also be found as brushstroke groupings. Yellow crosshatching may be used.

b. Duplication (or variation) of the design on the trunk front.

c. <u>Four red units or rope stroke with yellow and/or green brushstroke groupings.</u>

d. Floral spray with three large red blossoms. Alizarin and white brushstroke group overtones and yellow crosshatching. Green and yellow leaflets on yellow stems. Large veined leaves may also be found.

A6. Trunk Lids:

   a. Yellow strokes painted as ribbon, rope, brushstroke groupings, and occasionally dots.

   b. White berries may be used at base of yellow groupings.
   c. Red border strokes used along with yellow ones.
   d. Red band with yellow or black overpainting occasionally found around the outer edge of lid.

A7. Striping:

   a. Yellow striping on the lid. Occasionally done in red.
   b. Striping forms a closed rectangle and stripe lines do not extend to outer edges of lid.
   c. Stripes are occasionally found on trunk front or end.

Group III—Section B

B1. Background: Asphaltum or black.

B2. Designs: Geometrically balanced. <u>Green color seldom found.</u>

B3. Painted Bands:

    a. Red or blue color.

    b. Straight or swagged. Swags may be scalloped on lower edge as seen under Group III—Section A.

    c. Overtones on bands—

        1.) Alternating alizarin, white, and/or blue (in any combination) on red band.

        2.) Red and white brushstroke groups on blue band.

    d. Yellow squiggles as seen under Group I—Section B may be used under swags.

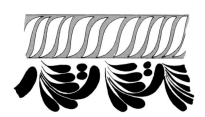 

B4. Trunk Lids: Ribbon stroke (yellow or blue) around the edge with brushstroke groups (yellow or red) in corners and at handle, as seen in Group I—Section B.

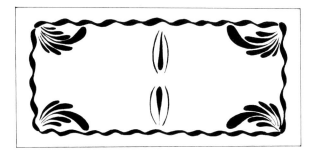 

 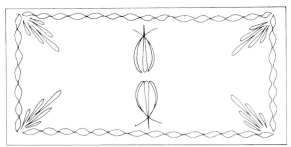

B5. Trunk Ends: One-half of the design that appears on the front.

B6. Borders: Yellow ribbon stroke. Occasionally it is a tiny compact ribbon as seen in Group II.

B7. Striping: Seldom found.

Group III—Section C

C1. Background: Asphaltum or black.

C2. Design: Geometrically balanced floral spray.

C3. Flowers:
- a. Two large flowers with smaller bud forms, showing similarities to the trunk ends under Group III—Section A.
- b. Alizarin and white overtones painted as brushstroke groupings, alternating crescent-shaped strokes or in crosswise direction as seen under Group III—Section A.
- c. Red stems.

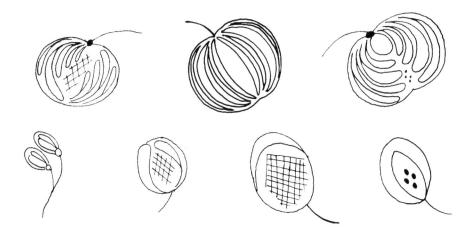

C4. Leaves:
- a. Yellow and green leaflets along the stem.
- b. Large rounded leaves (usually three) near base end of stems.

C5. Lid Facing Edge: Either <u>no decoration</u> or yellow ribbon stroke.

C6. Trunk Lids: similar to Group III—Section A.

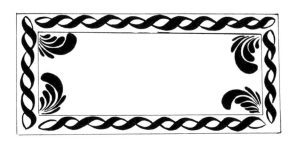

C7. Trunk Ends:

    a. <u>Single round red flower</u> as seen under Group III—Section A.

    b. <u>Four red units</u> as seen under Group III—Section A.

    c. Yellow ribbon stroke forming a large X.

C8. Striping: Occasionally found on lid in yellow paint.

Trunk Fronts

GROUP IV

The first three pieces (Figs. 1.39a, 1.39b, and 1.40) are the type of construction considered to be of English origin. It seems feasible to believe that Edward Pattison would have made the tinware styles with which he was familiar, and would also have trained others to produce these shapes. Tin knife trays of this style did not seem to be popular with the Americans, and their scarcity today indicates that they were not long in production. Bread basket styles also changed to suit the taste of the American buyers.

Fig. 1.39a and 1.39b. Knife Trays 14½" (36.8 cm). Black. A painted white band adorns the upper rim of these two knife trays. Alternating groups of red and blue-green brushstrokes with green dots are added to the band in Fig. 1.39a. A wide yellow stripe edges the band and there is a narrow scallop, or lattice, below it. A row of single yellow brushstrokes separated by two dots edges the floor. Fig. 1.39b shows large blue-green 'S' strokes with two red strokes between each. This piece has had some restoration.

Collections of Rebecca Roure (deceased) and Olive Brandt

Fig. 1.40. Bread basket 12½" (30.8 cm). Black. This white band is similar to Fig. 1.39b but with a double red stripe through its midline. Yellow rick rack and dots form the border below the band.

Collection of Martha Wilbur

Fig. 1.41. Snuffer tray 9⅛" (23.2 cm) Black. Blue-green strokes and red dot groups are painted on the white band. A yellow ribbon runs along the inner edge.

Collection of Phyllis Sherman

Fig. 1.42. Trunk 8½" (21.6 cm). Dark asphaltum. The white band on this trunk is overpainted with olive green and red groups, each separated by two vertical red lines. A narrow white band is also seen along the lower edge. Yellow rick rack and dots, as seen in Fig. 1.40, and a row of yellow brushstrokes are below the band. A large yellow rope, also similar to Fig. 1.40, runs along the lid face. Rows of various yellow strokes decorate the top and ends, and both red and yellow striping is used.

HSEAD Collection at The Museum of American Folk Art, New York, NY

Fig. 1.43a and 1.43b. Trunk 9⅝" (24.5 cm). Dark asphaltum. This trunk has two opaque white bands arched across the front with red flowers, buds, and stems. Olive green leaflets are used profusely, and green dots fill the openings in the blossoms. Two yellow lattices, similar

to those seen in Fig. 1.39a, fill the space between the two white bands. Below the arch are positioned brushstroke groups, rope stroke, and dots painted in yellow. Note the border on the lid face. Fig. 1.43b shows the trunk end with a signature of *Wm. Southard* (as yet unidentified).

Collection of Sherry Dotter

Fig. 1.44. Trunk 8⅝" (21.9 cm). Dark asphaltum. A straight white band with two matching units of red and olive green is painted across the front. Yellow stripes and graceful border strokes complete the decoration.

Collection of Sara Tiffany

Fig. 1.45. Trunk 7⅞" (20.0 cm). Black. A three-swag white band has floral sprays similar to Fig. 1.43a. A red stripe and yellow lattice edge each white swag, and yellow brushstroke groupings hang downward. Yellow rick rack is on the lid face and on the trunk ends forms an X. Striping and a yellow rope edge the lid.

Collection of Barbara Quirk

Fig. 1.46. Trunk 9¼" (24.4 cm). Black. White scallops are placed across the upper front of this trunk, and are overpainted with red star flowers and green leaflets. Green brushstroke groups are positioned along the edge of the white, and yellow groups descend down from the junctures. A straight white band edges each side of the trunk front, and berries and leaves are overpainted on it. The yellow border on the lid face was seen in Fig. 1.43a. The top, which is also similar to Fig. 1.43a, shows a large yellow rope with striping around the edge. Yellow ribbon strokes form an X on the ends.

Private Collection

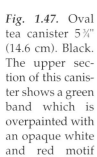

Fig. 1.47. Oval tea canister 5¾" (14.6 cm). Black. The upper section of this canister shows a green band which is overpainted with an opaque white and red motif that is very similar to Fig. 1.44. The top of the shoulder is edged by the yellow lattice as seen previously.

Anonymous

Fig. 1.48. 1-Sheet waiter 12⅜"(32.1 cm). Black. Around the floor of this waiter are graceful red and thin white brushstrokes overpainted on an olive green band. Note the extension and reverse curving of the red stroke. A yellow stripe and brushstroke border on the flange complete the design.

Collection of Zilla Lea (deceased)

Fig. 1.49. Trunk 9⅛" (23.2 cm). Dark asphaltum. Two identical flower units in red, yellow, and white are painted onto a soft blue band. Skillfully executed yellow brushstrokes border the band, the trunk ends, and the lid. The yellow lattice is positioned at the base edge. Note the larger strokes on the lid face which have a reverse curve as seen in Fig. 1.48.

Collection of Lois Tucker

Fig. 1.50. Trunk 9 ¼" (23.2 cm). Dark asphaltum. A narrow red band with "candy stripe" overtones edges three sides of the front. Eight red curls nestle along the band with yellow double crosshatching and dot groups filling the inner openings. Yellow brushstroke groups are positioned between the red curls. The front face border has been seen previously. (see Fig. 1.43)

Collection of Phyllis Sherman

Fig. 1.51a and 1.51b. Trunk 9 ⅝" (24.5 cm). Black. A red band forms an arch on the front of this trunk. We see for the first time in this group the use of alizarin, along with white, to accomplish the decoration on the band. The end has a red band with "candy stripe" overtones that were seen in Group III. Elaborate yellow borders are again seen. The yellow lattice is used on the front and the ends. Note the three yellow berries on stems hanging below the band on the trunk end.

HSEAD Collection at The Museum of American Folk Art, New York, NY

Fig. 1.52. Trunk 9 ⅛" (23.2 cm). Black. Large red units with green and white overtones adorn this trunk. Yellow crosshatching, brushstroke groups, and hash lines fill the open spaces. The end shows rows of yellow border strokes. The design in the top of the lid is very similar to Fig. 1.42.

Collection of Lois Tucker

Fig. 1.53. Trunk 9 ⅛" (23.2 cm) Black. This trunk has two narrow bands and six large swagged brushstrokes painted in a soft blue. Both white and red are used for overpainting. Red lines form rectangles between the two bands, and these are filled with brushstroke groups in yellow and white. Double crosshatching and dots fill the spaces above each swag. Yellow groups and squiggles decorate below the swags.

Collection of Ingrid Pomeroy

Fig. 1.54a and 1.54b. Trunk 9⅛" (23.2 cm). Asphaltum. Three broad red swags, positioned below a red ribbon, span the front of this trunk. Alizarin and white are used for overtones. Yellow brushstroke groups nestle above the swags and also hang down between them. Tight yellow rick rack edges the lower part of each swag. The lid shows a large rope stroke and double striping. Note that this border is not painted along the back edge of the lid. The strokes around the handle are the same as seen in Fig. 1.50.

Collection of Marianne Hauck

Fig. 1.55a and ***1.55b.*** Trunk 7" (17.8 cm). Black. Two red swags with "candy striped" overtones, along with yellow brushstroke groups, decorate this trunk front. The lid face border is the same as on the floor of Fig. 1.39a. The back shows a wreath painted around initials (probably of the owner).

Anonymous

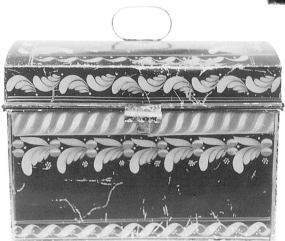

Fig. 1.56. Trunk 9⅜" (24.4 cm). Black. An expertly painted trunk with a red band above a row of berries and yellow leaves.

Private Collection

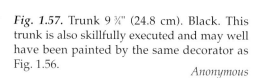

Fig. 1.57. Trunk 9¾" (24.8 cm). Black. This trunk is also skillfully executed and may well have been painted by the same decorator as Fig. 1.56.

Anonymous

Group IV

1. Background: Asphaltum or black.

2. Designs: Geometrically balanced.

3. Painted Bands (in various shapes):
    a. White Bands—overpainted with red and green (transparent or opaque).
    b. Red Bands—overpainted with alizarin and white. Occasionally green and white.
    c. Green Bands—overpainted with red and white. Sometimes also yellow.
    d. Blue Bands—overpainted with red and white. Sometimes also yellow.

4. Overtones:
    a. Brushstoke groupings.
    b. Large rope stroke.
    c. Spray of red flowers or berries with single stroke green leaflets.
    d. Alizarin and white "candy striping" arrangements.

Painted Bands

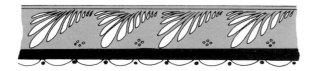

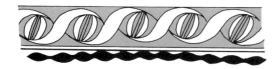

Painted Bands

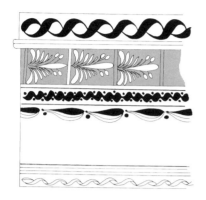 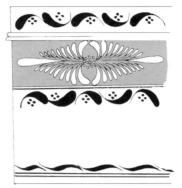 

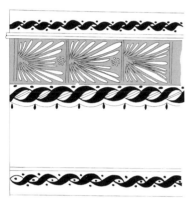  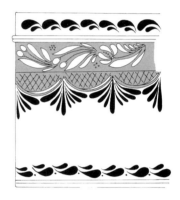

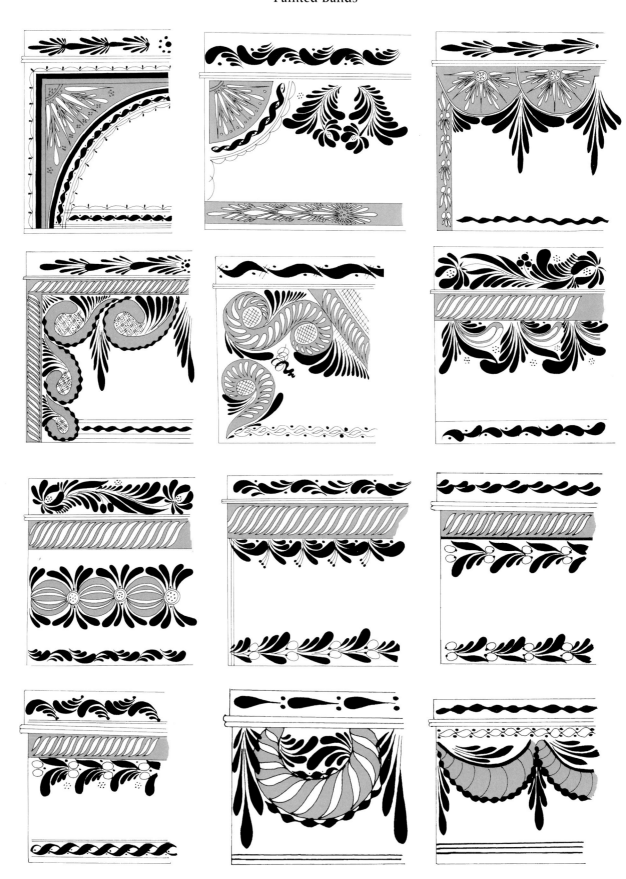

5. Borders:

    a. Large variety of strokes, usually painted in yellow.

    b. Scalloped yellow line with tear drop stroke at junctures.

    c. Trunk lids— strokes painted along stripe lines.

    d. Trunk ends—usually horizontal rows of border strokes. Occasionally a continuation of a design from the trunk front.

6. Striping:

    a. Usually yellow in single or double lines.

    b. Striping lines extend to outer edges of lid.

Trunk Ends

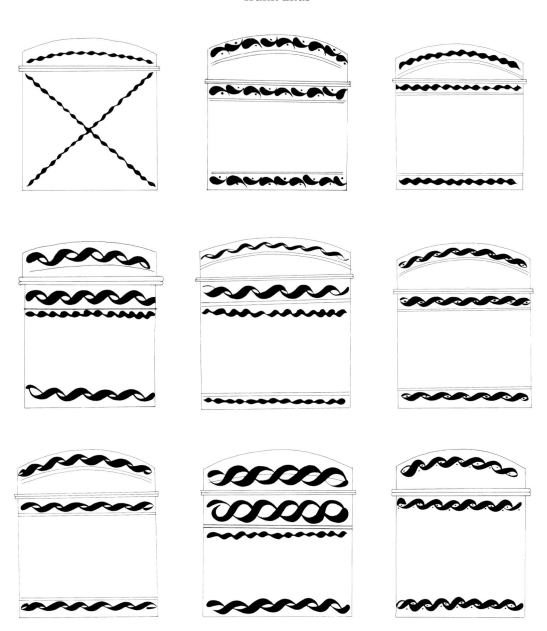

Trunk Ends

Trunk Lids

Trunk Lids

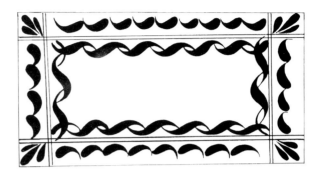

Chapter Two

THE UPSON TINSHOP
[circa 1773–1837]
Marion [Southington], Connecticut

J ames Upson [1756—1803] served his apprenticeship (possible dates: 1768—1773) in the tinshop of Edward Pattison. Upon completion of his training, his father, Josiah Upson [1721—1806] built a tinshop for his promising young son about a hundred yards from the family home. It opened about 1773 and James took into partnership an experienced tinman, Josiah Cowles [1716—1793], one of Pattison's first apprentices. Josiah had become a proficient tinsmith in that shop. James, like most tinsmiths, was also engaged in farming. He had acquired the family farm through purchase and inheritance.

Quinnipac Cemetery marker in Southington:

James Upson died Oct. 22, 1803, Aged 46. Mary, his wife died Sept. 2, 1842, Aged 84.

When the Revolutionary War broke out, all tinshops were forced to close because supplies of tinplate from Wales were no longer available. James enlisted and served a year during the war. After he returned home, he enlarged the shop and his profitable business resumed. In 1781 he married Mary Cowles, his partner's daughter. They had two sons, Asahel [1781—1867] and (James) Salmon [1791—1874]. Salmon never used the name "James", even on legal papers. After his father-in-law's death in 1793, James Upson continued to operate the shop. When he died, the shop passed to his son, Asahel. At first, the business was managed by a grandson of Josiah Cowles, also named Josiah. When Asahel and Salmon were older and sufficiently trained to carry on the trade, they assumed the management.

The tinshop of James Upson

Wonx Springs
Cemetery stone:

*Asahel Upson died June 14,
1867, Aged 84.*

Asahel, who lived and died on the family homestead, married Lydia Webster [1781—1861] of Plantsville in 1806, and raised a family of nine sons.

Salmon Upson married first to Belinda Lewis [1789—1817], and in 1819 he married a decorator in his shop, Sarah Greenleaf [1798—1865] of Dorchester, Massachusetts. They had eight children, five of whom survived. Salmon, having sold to his brothers all his rights to the family homestead, built a house and tinshop about a mile away in Cheshire where he specialized in producing kitchen utensils, teapots, coffee pots, pitchers, and salt and pepper shakers. Salmon's son Elliot [1832—1915] was also a tinsmith. He joined the Meriden firm of Bradley, Hatch and Co. (later Bradley and Hubbard), and stayed in their employ for forty years.

Asahel and Salmon combined their production to meet orders that they shipped to the West, the South, and even to customers in England. Helen Rena Upson, the current family historian, tells of the October 1826 order placed to Asahel for 3085 pieces of tinware. This order consisted of dish kettles, tin quarts, ½ quarts, ½ gallons, pints, ½ pints, milkpans, round pans, basins, lantern pans, quart pans, grease pans, coffee pots, lanterns, graters, ½ shoats, canisters for powder, ½ pint scalloped pans, and candle molds. Although this assortment of tinware does not seem to be the type that might have been decorated, it was still a very sizable order and proof that the business was successful. The historian also notes that "Asahel and Salmon both seem not to have been producing after 1837, the time of financial panic that swept the country." Family letters reveal that Salmon was working at Mr. Bacon's tinshop in Middletown as late as 1845.

Five of Asahel's sons became involved in some aspect of the tin business. About 1830 Lauren [1807—1885] and James Robert [1809—1877] founded L & JR Upson & Co., a hardware firm located in Marion, Alabama. They received shipments of tinware from their father in Connecticut, along with various farm produce, and sent out peddlers to sell throughout the area. The banking crisis of the late 1830s caused them to eventually file for bankruptcy; however, Lauren relocated in Mobile and James in Jackson, Mississippi. Their new businesses were not as successful, and by 1850 they were engaged in other enterprises. Lauren studied law and was admitted to the bar. He also was editor of the Mobile Advertiser. Eventually he moved to California to become publisher of the Sacramento Union. James became interested in gold mining, and operated a store catering to the miners in Montana.

Dewitt Upson [1812—1879] was for a short time engaged with his brothers in Alabama but he returned to Connecticut. In partnership with N. Y. Otis, he established the Otis and Upson Clock Co., a firm that made cast iron clock cases with mother-of-pearl inlays. Warren Upson [1807—1835], the twin of Lauren [1807—1885], and Gad Ely [1823—1866] also joined their brothers in the South.

Asahel Augustus Upson [1816—1906] had worked with his father in the tinware business, and they made up a formula for japanning hardware. Asahel went South to join his brothers for a time, but by 1845 he had removed to Cincinnati, Ohio where business opportunities were excellent due to the influx of settlers along the Ohio River. He was associated with the George D. Winchell firm, a very successful manufacturer of japanned ware. The company made a great variety of items, such as tea caddies, toy whistles, knife trays, trunks, lamps, and candlesticks. They also made large extensively decorated water coolers. The merchandise was pressed by machine, and in 1850 the firm processed 1200 boxes of tinplate. By 1870, 5000 boxes were processed.

About 1866 James Robert Upson returned to Connecticut and built a new house one hundred feet northwest of the Josiah Upson ancestral home. In the following generation this house became the home of his son Robert Ellsworth Upson [1863—1949] who married Helen Nickerson [1888—1976] in 1900. The very active Upson Family Association was founded in their home in 1925 and Helen became the family historian. Through her timely research this family's history has been preserved.

Prepared by Mona D. Rowell and Lois Tucker

Cheshire Street Cemetery markers:
Sarah Greenleaf, wife of Salmon Upson, died Jan. 29, 1865,
Aged 66. Salmon Upson died April 14, 1874, Aged 81 yrs 8 mos.

UPSON SHOP: Introduction to the Photographs

The Upson tinshop began to decorate tinware and employ local women for this work in 1800. A tin trunk from the Upson family was included in a collection of Upson tinshop tools that was presented to Old Sturbridge Village in 1959 by Helen N. Upson in memory of her husband Robert Ellsworth Upson. In her research material Mrs. Upson wrote: "The Upson shop employed several talented young women to decorate many of the japanned products. One of these was Sarah Greenleaf of Dorchester who married young Salmon Upson, brother of Asahel, in 1819." Sarah was so proficient that she was put in charge of the other painters.

Apparently Sarah saved this trunk for her own use. Asahel's wife, Lydia, must have admired it greatly because, when she was very ill in 1861, Sarah gave it to her as a gift. Upon Lydia's death a few months later the trunk was given to Lydia's daughter-in-law, Mary [1837—1904], the mother of Robert Upson. Upon her death it became the proud possession of Robert's wife, Helen. According to family tradition, the trunk was decorated by Sarah Greenleaf Upson.

The study of the Upson Shop painted characteristics begins with this Upson family trunk (Fig. 2.1a and 2.1b). Characteristics found on this trunk are noted and explained. Proceeding to Fig. 2.2, similarities to Fig. 2.1 are pointed out and a new feature is introduced . This process of noting a new painted feature in conjunction with already identified features is continued through all the pictured examples.

After carefully studying and thoroughly analyzing each and every characteristic of the decoration on these pictured pieces as well as hundreds of others, a list of characteristics typical for this shop can be compiled. Such matters as the shapes of scalloped borders, the thickness and application styles of the paint, the colors and treatments of overlapping pigments, and the relationship of motifs on the front of a piece to the top or sides have all been taken into consideration.

Special thanks is given to Astrid Donnellan for discovering two of the following "signature marks" on an Upson trunk of her own. This in turn led to the discovery of many more of these marks on other pieces. The presence of the "signature" corroborated the design characteristics for the Upson shop.

Figure captions by Mona D. Rowell

Fig. 2.1a and 2.1b. Trunk 9" (23 cm). This Upson family piece serves as a key for identifying the painted tinware of this shop. It has an asphaltum background with two deep white swags on the front and a straight white band on each end. The large red scalloped single flower is typical for the shop. The center opening of the flower is accomplished by softening (with a finger) the edge of the wet red paint that is applied over the already dried white band, thus allowing the white band to show through. Note the stylized flowers, the two types of leaves (lobed and oval), and the fine black detail. A yellow brushstroke border is painted in thin yellow ochre and follows along the edge of the white banding. Often used is a row of double yellow brushstrokes along the upper edge of the trunk end. Important to note is a small circular black stroke with two tiny center strokes (in the lower part of right swag). Whether intended for a space filler or a signature is not known, but today we treat this as an identifying mark for this tin shop.

Old Sturbridge Village, Sturbridge, MA

Fig. 2.2a and 2.2b. Trunk 8 ⅜" (21.8 cm). Asphaltum background. This trunk is identified as an Upson piece since the design contains several of the units found in Fig. 2.1. Introduced here is a simple red peach with the suture formed by an alizarin overstroke, and a fine black stroke to accentuate the groove. Green brushstrokes represent the leaves. As in Fig. 2.1 there is a red stripe on the lower edge of the straight white band.

Collection of Marion Matthews (deceased)

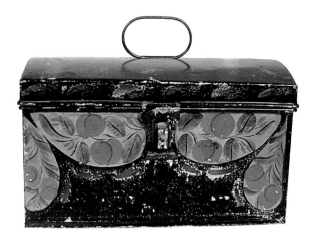

Fig. 2.3. Trunk 8 ⅜" (21.4 cm). Asphaltum. White swags and bands were very popular in this shop, with many quite unusual, as seen here. Red berries, scattered among peaches and green leaves, are painted on the band. Stripes, borders, and brushwork on trunk lids are often badly worn.
Collection of Jessica Bond

Fig. 2.4. Round canister 7 ⁵⁄₁₆" (18.5 cm). Asphaltum. A simple rose motif with thin alizarin brushstrokes (barely discernible) and fine black detail. Unfortunately the "identifying mark" is hidden under the hasp. Canisters are usually decorated on the front only with simple brushstroke borders on the top, bottom, and vertically on each side.

Old Sturbridge Village, Sturbridge, MA

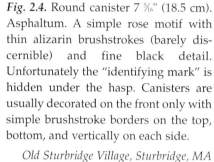

Fig. 2.5. Match Holder 7 ½" (19 cm). Asphaltum. Here is shown a simple red flower on a white swag. Large green leaves show a curved black stroke which gives the effect of the leaf edge turning over. Note the series of red and yellow brushstrokes around the hang hole.

HSEAD Collection at Museum of American Folk Art, New York, NY

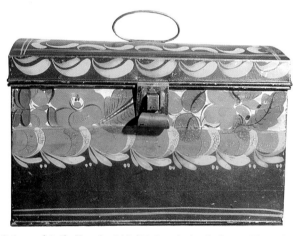

Fig. 2.6a and 2.6b. Trunk 8 ½" (21.6 cm). Asphaltum. The white band shows an open-centered flower and smaller buds. On the trunk end are stylized flowers that have petals formed by a scalloped alizarin stroke which has been "fingered off" on one edge as described in Fig. 2.1. Notice the scalloped red band below the white band. The curves of this band are accented by a large alizarin stroke and several yellow strokes.
Anonymous

Fig. 2.7. Trunk 6¼" (15.8 cm). Asphaltum. Variations of the lobed flower painted on the white swags are used in other shops. Note the yellow and black at the base of the red flower. An opaque chrome yellow is used on the borders. The series of graduated brushstrokes on the ends of the lid are typical for this shop, but the sunburst unit around the handle is found in other tinshops.

Collection of Ethel Holmes (deceased)

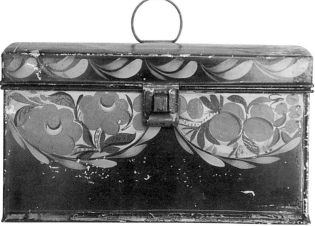

Fig. 2.8. Trunk 8¾" (22.2 cm). Asphaltum. The flowers on the swagged white band have a central opening containing black and yellow strokes. Red dots form the stems. Peaches and cherries are also seen.

Collection of Sandra Strong

Fig. 2.9. Trunk 9⅛" (23.2 cm). Asphaltum. There was a tendency among the Upson painters to use very thin paint, especially so with green and alizarin. Having faded over the years, it is still often visible on the white bands but not always on the darker background color. The white fruit is given shape with vermillion overstrokes which have been "fingered off". Note the more elongated leaf of the end of trunk, and also the blue green color used. This trunk has a white band only on the ends. The "identifying mark" is located at the far end.

Collection of Astrid Donnellan

Fig. 2.10. Flat-topped Box 10¾" (27.3 cm). Asphaltum. This unusual box has a straight white band around the edge of the cover. The flowers, buds, and leaves painted on the band have been previously seen, and there is a cluster of grapes. The design on the front of this box has opaque white flowers given form by red strokes that have been fingered-off. Buds are shown, as well as oval green leaves with black veining.

Collection of Astrid Donnellan

Fig. 2.11. Trunk 8 ⅝" (21.9 cm). Asphaltum. The bands on this piece exhibit the same motifs previously seen but notice the shape and color of the leaves. The two ends of the trunk are different, with two simple flowers that have open centers on one and two peaches on the other.

Collection of Gail Gaglio

Fig. 2.12. Match holder 7 ½" (19 cm). Asphaltum. The single scalloped flower introduces shading done first with vermillion which is then shaded with alizarin. There is a green stroke below the center dot. The spray at the top consists of two buds with a yellow dot at the end.

Collection of Margaret Willey (deceased)

Fig. 2.13a and 2.13b. Trunk 8 ⅝" (21.8 cm). Asphaltum. White bands on the end show the typical peaches. Note the border below the band. The front design consists of a single white flower, a white morning glory, and two large buds—all with the "fingered off" shading. Note the red dots as accents and the triangular group representing stamens.

Anonymous

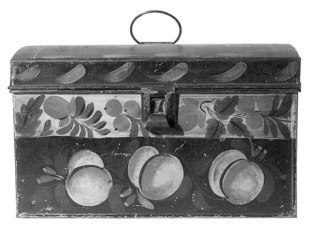

Fig. 2.14. Trunk 8 ⅝" (22 cm). Asphaltum. A straight white band with three large white peaches below it adorns this trunk. "Fingered-off" accents in both red and yellow give shape to the peaches.

Collection of Ruth Coggins (deceased)

Fig. 2.15a and 2.15b. Trunk 9 ¾" (24.7 cm). Asphaltum. A more elaborate design than previously seen. The flower on the far right of the band is a new form. The morning glories have more detail, and show a series of red dots between the green sepals. Groups of red and greyish-blue grape clusters are used. Note that the white band on the trunk end is scalloped.

Courtesy, Ohio Historical Society, Columbus, OH

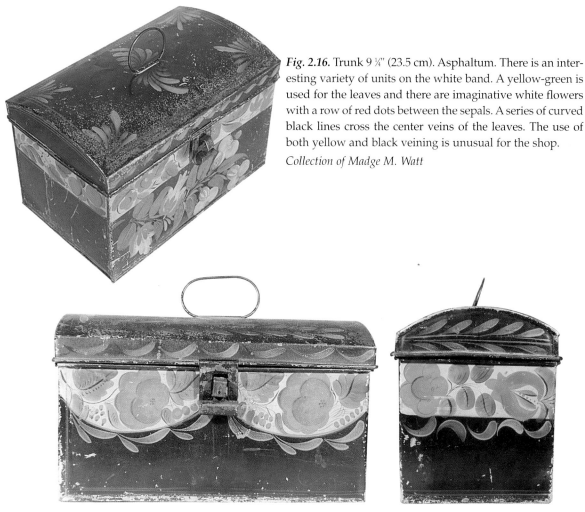

Fig. 2.16. Trunk 9 ¼" (23.5 cm). Asphaltum. There is an interesting variety of units on the white band. A yellow-green is used for the leaves and there are imaginative white flowers with a row of red dots between the sepals. A series of curved black lines cross the center veins of the leaves. The use of both yellow and black veining is unusual for the shop.

Collection of Madge M. Watt

Fig. 2.17a and 2.17b. Trunk 8 ¾" (22.2 cm). Asphaltum. Red roselike flowers with thin alizarin brushstrokes giving shape and an unusual imaginative flower are seen on the end band.

Collection of Sara Tiffany

Fig. 2.18. Apple Basket 12 ½" (31.8 cm). Asphaltum. The flowers and leaves on the band are now familiar. A new feature is the yellow band with a superimposed wavy black line painted around the floor.

Collection of Laura Corvini

Fig. 2.19. Apple basket 11" (28 cm). Asphaltum. The white band shows the now familiar red peaches separated by green leaves with red dot center stems.

Collection of Sherry Dotter

Fig. 2.20. One-sheet waiter 12 ⅝" (32.1 cm). Asphaltum on crystallized tin. Note that the white band is painted in four sections and not continuous around the floor of the tray. Similar corner motifs are generally found when the bands are executed in this manner.

Collection of Ruth Carter

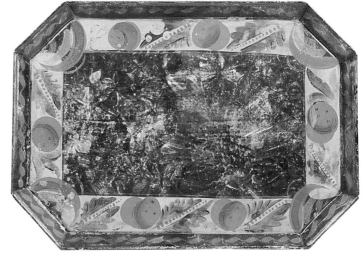

Fig. 2.21. Bread basket 13⅜" (33.9 cm). Asphaltum on crystallized tin. The white band is on the end sections only and shows units previously seen. The yellow brushstroke arrangement below the band is sometimes found on Upson trunks as well. The use of alternating yellow and red strokes along the sides of this piece is not unique to this shop, nor is the yellow band with the serpentine black line.

Collection of Peg Watts

Fig. 2.22. Bread basket 14⅛" (35.7 cm). Asphaltum. Round white flowers and buds are shaped with scalloped petals. Yellow leaf veining is not often seen in the Upson shop.

Collection of Arlene Lennox (deceased)

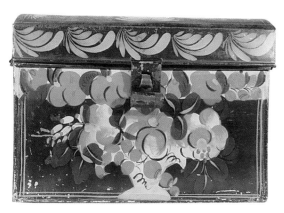

Fig. 2.23a and 2.23b. Trunk 9¾" (24.8 cm). Asphaltum.. This design shows similarities with the previously shown examples, but is more complex in the arrangement of the flowers in a white urn. Some veins are yellow. The full brushstroke border on the lid front was often found on the larger pieces. The brush work on the top in which brushstroke clusters form flowers along the stripe line is another unique feature of this shop.

Collection of Maryellen O'Toole

Fig. 2.24a and 2.24b. Boxes 4" (10.1 cm). Upson pieces in general have asphaltum backgrounds; however, these small boxes are most often decorated on a white ground. Asphaltum or dark green backgrounds may also be found. Simple sprays appear twice on the front and usually once on the ends, while a fuller design is on the top of the lid. The boxes had many uses and even stove polish was sold in them.

Collections of Charlotte Paddock (deceased) and Private Collection.

Fig. 2.25a. Trunk 4 ¼" (10.7 cm). Yellow. *Fig. 2.25b.* Trunk 2 ¾" (7 cm). Red. These small dome-topped trunks show simple repeat motifs like those in Fig. 2.24. They may also be found with white backgrounds.

Collections of Virginia Wheelock and Anononymous

Fig. 2.26a and 2.26b. Box 6 ½" (16.5 cm) White. This small flat-topped box has a different floral spray on each side. Vermilion roses and buds, along with thin blue-grey flowers, are seen.

Collection of Dortia Davis

CHARACTERISTICS OF UPSON SHOP DECORATION

The following illustrations demonstrate in greater detail than the preceding photographs the characteristics of design found in the Upson Shop. The dotted lines shown in some flowers and fruit drawings indicate that the particular pigment (whether a base paint or an overtone color) has been fingered off in that area.

Colors found on Upson pieces:

Reds — orange vermilion, vermilion, cadmium red light, or vibrant bright red.

Greens — dark olive, bluish green, or grassy green (semi-transparent or opaque).

Yellow — chrome medium or lemon (semi-transparent, sometimes opaque).

White and alizarin overtones (thin pigment).

White bands — opaque.

Blue — transparent or opaque.

Black — used for accents and detail painting.

Types of decorated tinware found:

Trunks — dome-topped in various sizes

Trunks — flat-top, small sizes

Trunks — large, square, flat-topped with brass handles (Rare!)

Bread Basket

Apple Basket

Canisters

Waiters — 1-sheet and 2-sheet

Matchsafes

Tea Canister (round)

Round dish, small size

Illustration selections and line drawings by Gina Martin and Lois Tucker

Note: All six "signature marks" appear on one trunk.

Refer to page xv for the guide to interpretation of the line drawings.

1. Backgrounds: Asphaltum; some crystallizing (small stove polish boxes have been found with red, green, yellow, and white backgrounds).

2. Flowers and Fruits:
   a. Red or white.
   b. Many shapes found but few are based on simple brushstroke-form. Many flowers with scalloped outer edge.
   c. Open centers in the flowers very common.
   d. Morning glories.
   e. White flowers and fruits have red petals or accents applied on them with much fingering-off technique. In turn the red often has alizarin applied which is then fingered-off.
   f. Peaches, berries, pears, grapes, and cherries.
   g. Shell motifs.
   h. Overtones on red motifs in alizarin, either fingered-off or applied as single brushstrokes rather than clusters. Often shaped with a scalloped edge.
   i. White overtones are sometimes heavy.
   j. Yellow overtones with some fingering-off.
   k. Transparent blue overtones sometimes used on white flowers.
   l. Black accents (dots, lines, and the "signature" marks).
   m. Green accents used on white flowers.
   n. Stamens in red, white, or both in a triangular shape used on flowers.

Red Flowers

White Flowers

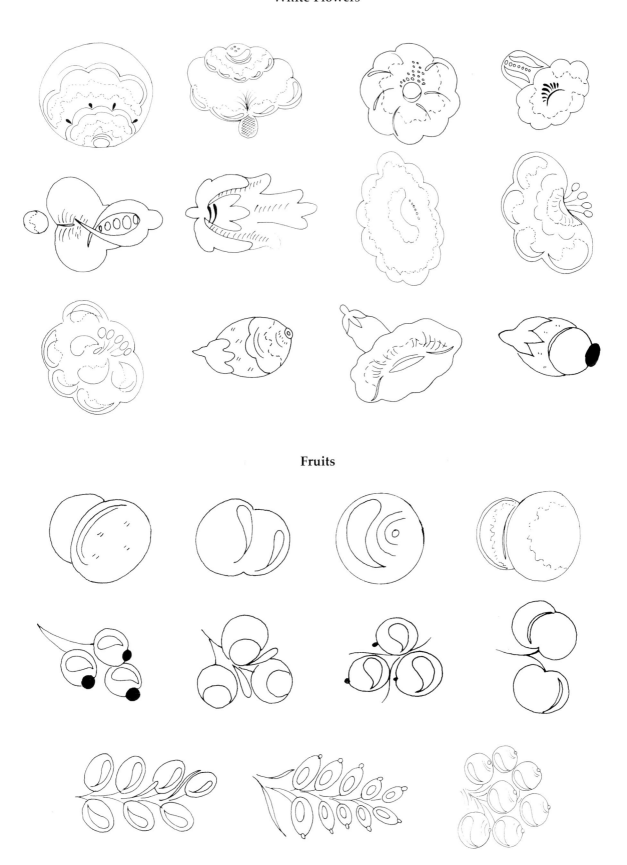

Fruits

Fruits

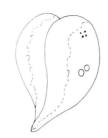

3. Leaves:

a. Large variety of shapes (note "signature" at far right.)

b. Black veining (occasional yellow center vein). Cross veins often formed with curved lines.

c. <u>Turn-over at the tip (formed by a black curved line).</u>

d. <u>Split leaf with the center vein comprised of row of red dots</u> (<u>sometimes with black accents</u>).

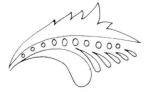

4. Trunk Fronts:

   a. Opaque white bands (straight, swagged, scalloped, or draped).

Straight White Bands

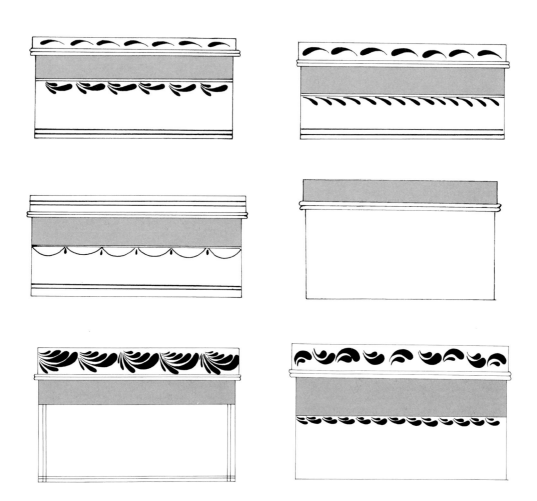

Swagged White Bands

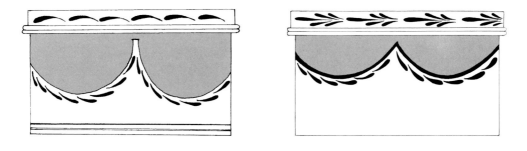

Scalloped White Bands

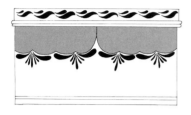 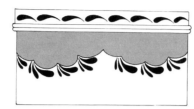 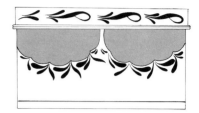

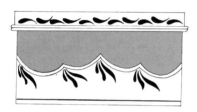  

Draped White Bands

 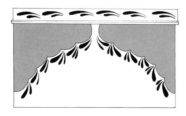 

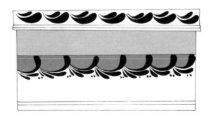

Unusual example with a scalloped red band below a straight white band.

4. Trunk Fronts

b. Sprays of white flowers or white fruits, either beneath a white band
   —OR— with no white band at all.

This example has the white band on the front face of the lid.

5. Flat-topped Round Canisters. The white band covers only the front section, and it ends at the side seams of the canister. Brushstroke borders adorn the front face of the lid, the lower edge of the band usually, and vertically along the side seam.

6. Trunk Lids:

a. Single or double stripes crossed over at the corner on trunks. (Stripes are usually not crossed.)

 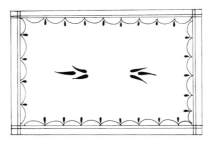 

b. Scalloped line with "teardrop" strokes at the junctures.

c. <u>Brushstroke clusters often form a flower along the stripe line, and the strokes on one side may be larger than those on the other.</u> Brushstrokes curved and are largest in the center of the group.

7. Trunk Ends:

a. Brushstroke arrangements similar to those on the lids.

b. No white bands.

c. White band (straight) in conjuncture with front bands that may be other than straight.

d. White band in swags or scallops.

e. Brushstrokes on the upper edge of lid may be largest in the center of the grouping.

f. Brushstroke borders are usually in yellow, but sometimes are alternating red and yellow strokes.

No White Bands

Swagged White Bands

Scalloped White Bands

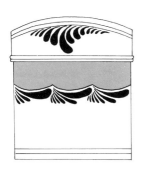   

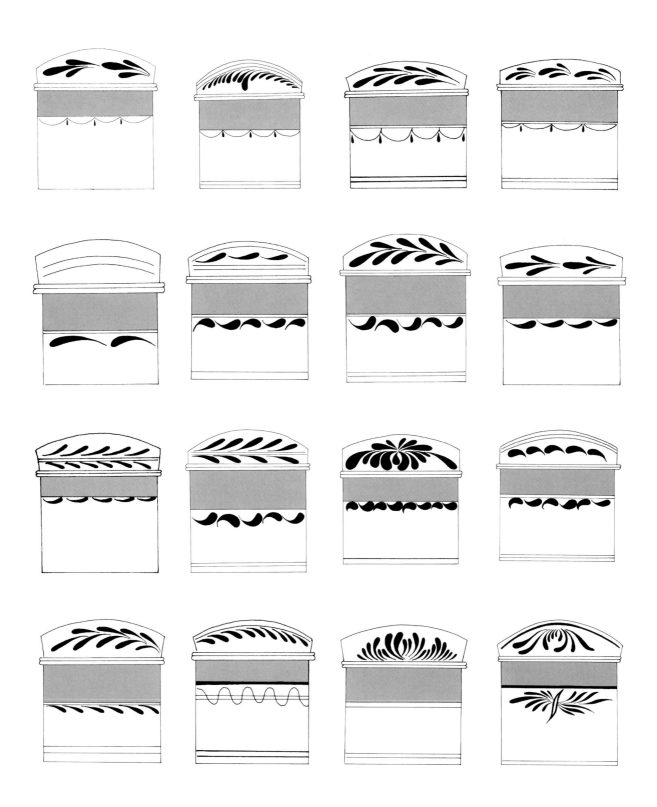

Straight White Bands

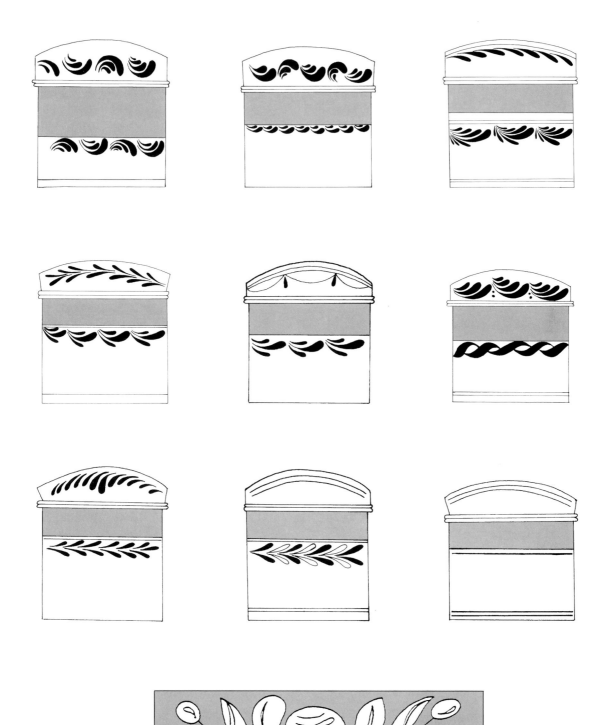

This motif often adorns a straight band on the end of trunks.

8. Striping:

    a. Red fine stripe usually on lower edge of straight or swagged white bands.

    b. Yellow stripe usually on lower edge of scalloped white band.

    c. Double fine stripes usually on lids and along the base edges.

    d. Yellow ¼" band with a fine black wavy line painted in it.

Additional Brushstroke Border Designs used in the Upson Tinshop

Chapter Three

THE NORTH TINSHOP
[circa 1790–1841]
Fly Creek, New York

The North families of Berlin, Connecticut played an important role in the development of several businesses associated with metal manufacturing, including blacksmithing, pistol making, tinsmithing and toolmaking.

It is believed that Jedediah North [1734—1816], a blacksmith, trained two of his sons in the trade: Levi [1760—1846] and Simeon [1765—1852], who later turned to making pistols. Levi's son, also named Jedediah [1789—1855], who was no doubt trained by his father, completed his apprenticeship as a blacksmith and went into business in 1810 or 1811. Later he began to concentrate on making tinner's hand tools. The company's account books reveal that orders were received from tinsmiths in almost every state east of the Mississippi, attesting to the fact that Jedediah was well known and considered a first-rate toolmaker.

Stephen North [1767—1842], the fifth son of the elder Jedediah, completed his apprenticeship as a tinsmith and in 1788 married Susannah Savage. After the birth of their son Albert in 1789, they moved to Fly Creek, New York, a small village northwest of Cooperstown, and there opened a tinshop.

As the turnpikes began to open up, many young families emigrated west into New York State, often attracted to areas where relatives or friends had already relocated or where active groups of the same religious persuasion had settled. Among them were many North cousins. In 1853 Linus North wrote from Palmyra to his uncle Jedediah for punches

and added to his letter: "We have, you see, a little society of cousins and all appear to love religion so that we spend some of our time agreeably." The 1790 Federal Census listed 92 North families in this country with 33 in Connecticut and 18 in New York State.

It seems reasonable to assume that Stephen's wife Susannah learned to paint tinware in Berlin as did other young girls of the community, especially since she and her husband were planning to move to a new area and establish a tinshop. No doubt their nine children had training in some phase of the business. Albert and Linus both worked in the tin business. Stephen Jr. was a tin and iron merchant in Jonesville, Michigan. Orrin was a merchant in Lockport, New York and Cincinnati, Ohio and he eventually moved to Michigan. Emily died in her early twenties. Almira, Mercy, Hepzibah and Susannah married and moved to neighboring towns. Susannah Savage North died in 1833 and Stephen married again to Matilda Cheney by whom he had three more daughters–Anne, who died in infancy, and twins Sarah and Mary.

Albert [1789—1849], Stephen's oldest son, became a tinsmith. He married Irena Taylor in 1811 and in time assumed most of the responsibility for the North tinshop and general store, judging by advertisements that appeared in the *Freeman's Journal* of Cooperstown. Two in 1825 read: "A general assortment of Plain and Japanned Tin, wholesale or retail, to suit the purchaser. Philadelphia stoves also sold." and "Tin, sheet iron and copperwork done in the best manner." In April 1840 an advertisement read: "Also on hand an extensive assortment of Plain and Japanned Tin which will be sold to Merchants, Pedlars or Farmers. A. North & Son." Albert's son Ceylon [1811—1879] worked with him until the shop closed in 1841.

Linus [1794—1846], Stephen's second son, married Justa Maria Fitch. He studied at the Auburn Theological Seminary and became a Presbyterian minister. His health was poor, however, and he eventually lost his voice. Although he continued with ministerial duties such as performing marriages, he was no longer able to preach. By 1823 he moved to Palmyra and set up a tinware business. In one of his letters he explained "I am establishing a shop for tin, sheet iron and patent combs in connection with one of my brothers-in-law. This place promises a good support for business." An advertisement in the *Wayne Sentinel* for November 1823 tells of the new establishment of Linus North and Alanson Pierson. They offered for sale plain and japanned tinware "superior in quality to that usually manufactured in this state." They also were offering to the public stove pipe, still boilers, writing paper, school books, tobacco, snuff, Scotch, lamp oil, turpentine, copal varnish and gum. This business seems to have been short-lived as a notice in the July 1824 *Sentinel* describes the dissolution of the partnership. The same paper has an advertisement for Hook's Patent Flax Machine placed by A. Pierson and Co. In October of

Fly Creek Cemetery:

"In memory of Elder Stephen North who was born in Berlin Conn Jan. 26, 1767. Died at Fly Creek NY Jan 11, 1842."

the same year, Pierson advertises a sale of the merchandise "at the old stand of North and Pierson."

There is very little information concerning the decoration and painters in this shop. It is assumed that the girls in the family painted the tinware until they married and moved away. In correspondence with his cousin Jedediah, the toolmaker, Albert asked him to send one of his eight sisters to Fly Creek and added: "I think I can occupy her leisure hours at Painting" which suggests that they all were painters. The Betsy North on the shop's payroll was most likely Jedediah's daughter. All branches of the family were very religious and had very strong family ties.

Prepared by Mona D. Rowell and Lois Tucker

NORTH SHOP: Introduction to the Photographs

The bread basket in Figure 3.1 is the only signed North piece that has been found in this study. It is signed by Mercy North [1798–1872], a daughter of Stephen and Susannah. There was a second Mercy North, the wife of a tinsmith in Elmira, New York, living at the same time. It is, however, reasonable to attribute this bread basket to the Mercy of Fly Creek since a large number of pieces of similar design are still in existence a century and a half later. This would lead one to believe that they were made and decorated in a large and productive shop. Since Mercy did not marry until she was 26 years old, she could have painted much tinware for the shop and may even have been in charge of decorating.

Using this bread basket as a key, it is possible to identify various types of decoration used in the North shop by careful examination and comparison of motifs, style, quality, paint color and consistency. From this a systematic relationship has been developed for the collection of photographs that follow. The types of decoration for the North shop are divided into three groups.

Worthy of mention here is a specific brushstroke shaped like a soup ladle. It is used extensively by this tinshop and will be referred to throughout the chapter as the "ladle" stroke. This stroke is a smaller version of that seen in Figs. 1.48 and 1.49, and is another indication of Berlin training for this tinsmith.

Figure captions by Mona D. Rowell and Lois Tucker

GROUP I

Fig. 3.1. Bread basket 8" x 12⅜" (20.3 x 31.3 cm). Asphaltum. The piece is signed in yellow paint *Mercy North* on the floor of the basket next to the crease on the long side. This particular piece of tin was manufactured in England. Along the upper edge is a white band on which is superimposed a continuous border type design of small red brushstroke flowers on a red stem. There are transparent alizarin overtones and large green leaves. The leaves show darker green centers and fine yellow lines accentuating the lobes. Below this band is a border comprised of yellow "ladle" strokes with a circle of yellow dots between each. The floor decoration of the basket is another continuous border design comprised of white brushstroke flowers on a red stem. They have opaque red overtones and green leaflets.

New York State Historical Association, Cooperstown, NY

Fig. 3.2. Trunk 8½" (21.6 cm). Mottled asphaltum. The design on the white band is painted in the same manner as in Fig. 3.1. Circles of small green dots fill the spaces around the flowers. Note the unusual line of red dots along the lower edge of the band. Large red rope-like strokes with transparent alizarin and white overtones form a border below the band. Yellow dot circles are found in the openings as seen in Fig. 3.1. A third border design runs along the base edge and consists of a white stroke which is overpainted with red and green, flanked by groups of yellow strokes. It is typical for the North border designs to be painted in many different colors. The tops of trunk lids are often badly worn even though the rest of the piece may be well preserved. Many have very large brushstrokes in either red, white or yellow in front and in back of the handle. These will be surrounded by groups of green or yellow strokes. Note that the floral vine on the painted band on both the left and right sides flows from the back edge of the trunk, around the front corner and across one half of the front to the hasp. There is no break in the design to allow for rounding the corners of the trunk. The rope border as well as the base edge border are treated in the same manner.

New York State Historical Association, Cooperstown, NY

Fig. 3.3. Trunk 7¾" (19.7 cm). Mottled asphaltum. The design on the white band is similar to that on the floor of the piece in Fig. 3.1. Small berries are also included in the vine. Notice that the two center brushstrokes of the red flowers are very broad at their head end, a trait typical of this shop. The red rope border beneath the band has groups of green strokes nested along the upper and lower curves of the rope. The base edge border is the same as in Fig.3.2.

Collection of Peg Watts

Fig. 3.4. Trunk 7½" (19 cm). Mottled asphaltum. The opaque white band shows a vine of large and small red berries and transparent green leaflets along a red stem. This vine flows continuously from the back left side of the trunk across the entire front and around to the right side. The border below the band consists of large white rope strokes with red and green overstrokes, and groups of green strokes above and below the rope. The base edge border is two red berries separated by groups of green strokes that each have a yellow highlight.

Collection of Helene Britt

Fig. 3.5. Trunk 8 ⅝" (21.9 cm). Asphaltum. This white band, painted more thinly than previously seen, shows a vine similar to Fig.3.4. Below the band is a border design composed of very large white brushstrokes with red overstrokes and green dot circles. The white stroke has a group of green brushstrokes on the lower side and yellow ones on the upper side. The border at the base edge again shows the ladle-stroke. This time it is painted in red with groups of green strokes at the junctures. (This piece has been restored.)

State Museum of Pennsylvania, Harrisburg, PA

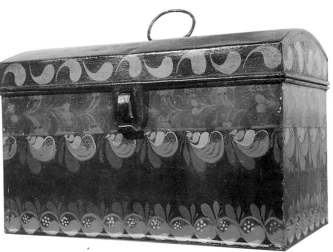

Fig. 3.6. Trunk 7¾" (19.7 cm). Mottled asphaltum. The painted bands for the North tinshop are most often straight along the lower edge. This piece, however, illustrates a scalloped band having a row of red dots along the edge. Yellow brushstrokes conform to the shape of the band. The base edge border is similar to Figs. 3.2 and 3.3, although it is now painted in red and green with groups of yellow dots. Notice that the trunk is missing its wire handle.

Private Collection

Mottling of the asphaltum background is a form of graining used on country painted tinware. It is accomplished by an additional application of asphaltum gently dabbed on, or sometimes dabbed and slightly dragged, with a wide irregularly edged brush. The dabbing is placed at intervals and may run horizontally, vertically, or diagonally, and covers the entire piece of tinware.

Fig. 3.7a and 3.7b. Trunk 8⅜" (21.9 cm). Mottled asphaltum. The white band on this piece is painted with groups of green leaflets on each side of a red stroke which extends from two red berries. The green strokes have black accent lines, and green dots and zigzag lines fill the areas between the groups. The design on this band is very similar to the base edge of Fig. 3.4. Striping along the lower edge of the band is usually done in red, but this trunk has a green stripe. Below the band is a green vine with white brushstroke flowers and berries that have opaque red strokes and green dots superimposed. Green leaflets along the red stems have a yellow highlight. The floral vine which is similar to Fig. 3.3, flows from left to right around the trunk. The top of the lid shows the "ladle" stroke painted along the edge, and there are brush-stroke groups in the four corners. The handle is surrounded by four yellow groups.

Anonymous

Fig 3.8. Trunk 8⅜" (21.9 cm). Mottled asphaltum. The band on this trunk is painted in red and adorned with a green rope design having yellow and black accents. Green brushstroke groups are nested along the rope, and there are white dots in the openings. The design below the band is nearly identical although it is painted with larger strokes in different colors. This rope border treatment was also seen in Figs. 3.3 and 3.4. The decoration on the top of the lid shows the "ladle" stroke painted in green around the outer edge. There are yellow dots in the spaces.

HSEAD Collection at the Museum of American Folk Art, New York, NY

Fig. 3.9. Trunk 8¾" (22.2 cm). Mottled asphaltum. This red band has repeating groups of green brushstrokes and green dot circles on each side of a transparent alizarin stroke. The flowing floral vine below the band again has red flowers with very broad center strokes as illustrated in Fig. 3.3. The decoration around the handle is similar to Fig 3.7b and is worked in red, green, and yellow.

Coffin Collection at the National Museum of American History, Washington, DC

Fig. 3.10. Oval Box 8 ¾" (21.3 cm). Mottled asphaltum. The red band has transparent "candy stripe" overtone strokes of alternating alizarin and white strokes. Below the band is a continuous vine with berries and leaves as seen in Fig. 3.4. The design across the front face of the lid shows a large red stroke with yellow strokes above and green strokes below it (see Fig. 3.5). The construction of this piece of tinware places the seam at the center back. This allows no natural stopping point for the decorator to end the design; therefore it was continued completely around the piece. Other tinshops constructed their oval boxes with a seam at each side, left and right, making it possible for the decorator to paint only on the front surface.

Collection of Deborah Lambeth

Fig. 3.11. Flour shaker 3 ⅞" (9.8 cm). Asphaltum. This decoration shows the "ladle" stroke painted in red along with three other simple borders. Note that the center border design does not meet up with itself after circling the shaker.

Collection of Margaret Willey (deceased)

Fig. 3.12a, 3.12b and 3.12c. Trunk 9 ¾" (24.8 cm). Mottled asphaltum. Although this trunk does not have bands and borders as shown in the previous illustrations, it still exhibits several of the characteristics seen in this group. The red flowers on the front and left end have the broad center strokes. Green brushstroke leaflets have a yellow highlight and yellow dot circles are used as fillers. A yellow rope border is used along the upper edge.

Collection of Anne E. Avery

CHARACTERISTICS OF NORTH SHOP DECORATION

The illustrations show the characteristics in greater detail than was possible with the photographs. Since the "ladle stroke" may be diffucult to discern in some drawings, it has been indicated with an arrow and marked "LS". Notations marked with a **[B]** depict a characteristic displaying strong influence of Berlin, Connecticut training.

Colors found on North pieces:
> Red–vermilion (occasionally orange vermilion or dark red)
> Green–medium, dark, olive
> Yellow–chrome medium (occasionally chrome light)
> White–opaque for bands, thin for overtones
> Alizarin–thin for overtones
> Blue–deep Prussian on white band

Types of decorated tinware found:
> Trunks (dome-topped in various sizes) were the main production of this shop. Only a few examples exist of other pieces of tinware, such as: flour dredger, 2-sheet waiter, oval dome-topped box, sugar bowl, and round tea canister.

Illustrations selected by Gina Martin and Lois Tucker
Line drawings by Lois Tucker

Group I (Mercy North)

Illustration of a section of the signed bread basket showing the "ladle" stroke and the signature.

*Refer to page xv for the guide to interpretation of the line drawings.

Group I (Mercy North):

1. Background: asphaltum (usually mottled).

2. White Bands: straight (occasionally scalloped) and continuing onto the ends of trunks or completely around oval boxes.

    a. Continuous vine of red brushstroke flowers or berries with alizarin overtones, red stems and green leaflets.
    b. Large repeating rope strokes in red or green with large red dots in the openings, and green brush-strokes along the curve.
    c. Green dot circles in flower centers and as space fillers.
    d. Red stripe along lower edge or occasionally a row of small red dots (one known example has a green stripe).

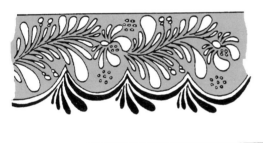

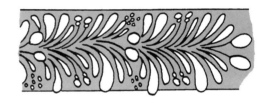

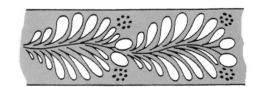

Group I (Mercy North):

3. Red Bands: straight and without a stripe.

     a. Continuous vine of brushstroke flowers painted in alizarin with green stems and leaflets.

     b. Green repeating rope stroke with green brushstrokes along the curves and white dots.

     c. Alternating alizarin and white "S" strokes in a candy-stripe manner **[B]**

     d. Green or alizarin dot circles.

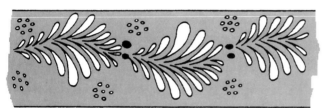

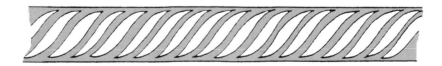

Group I (Mercy North):

4. Design directly under the band:

a. Vine of red or white brushstroke flowers like those found painted on the bands. Red flowers have alizarin and white overtones. White flowers have red overstrokes and green dots. Stems are red or green. Leaflets are green with or without yellow accents. Dot circles are yellow.

b. Extra large brushstrokes in red (with alizarin and white overtones) or white (with red overstrokes and green dots). Green and yellow (or just green) strokes around the large one.

c. Large repeating rope stroke in red (with alizarin and white) or white (with red and green). Yellow and green (or just green) brush strokes along curve of the rope stroke. Yellow dots in centers.

Designs placed below Red Bands

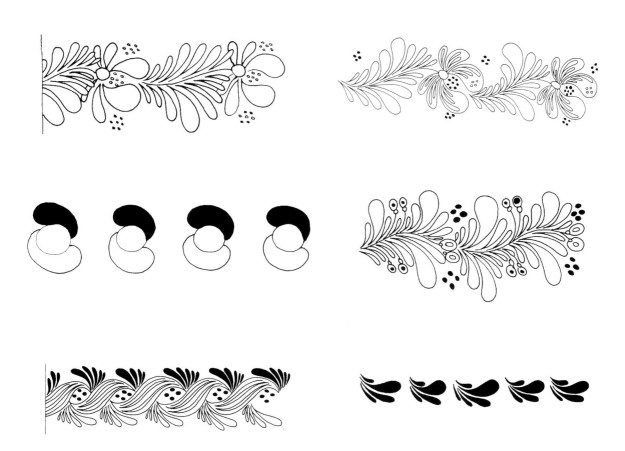

Group I (Mercy North):

Designs placed below White Bands

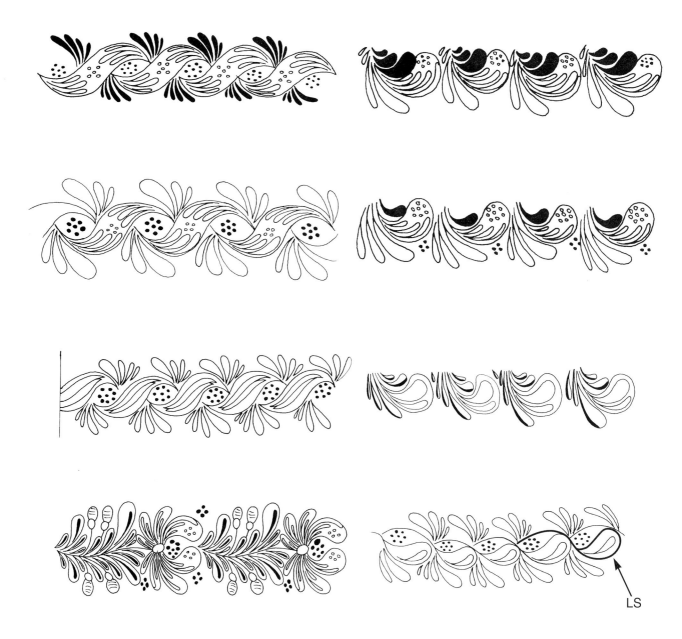

LS

Group I (Mercy North):

5. Flowers: <u>usually composed of 6, 8, or 10 brushstroke petals with the two center petals very wide at the head end.</u>

6. Floral spray design with no painted band:

    a. Red petaled flowers as well as buds.
    b. Green leaflets with yellow accents
    c. Large green leaves with yellow veins.
    d. Borders and lids as described under #7 and #8.

Floral Spray Designs

This trunk is a family piece owned by the descendants of Stephen North's son Albert.

Group I (Mercy North):

7. Borders along front face of lid and the base edge of trunk:

a. Cluster of brushstrokes with center stroke red (with alizarin and white overtones) or white (with red and green over strokes), and groups of green, yellow, or both on each side.

b. Two red berries with green or yellow brushstroke leaflets.

c. <u>"Ladle" stroke in red, yellow or green.</u> **[B]**

d. Yellow borders consisting of wide rick rack, "S" strokes, a row of dots, groups of three strokes and straight or curved brushstrokes.

Designs on Front Face of Lid

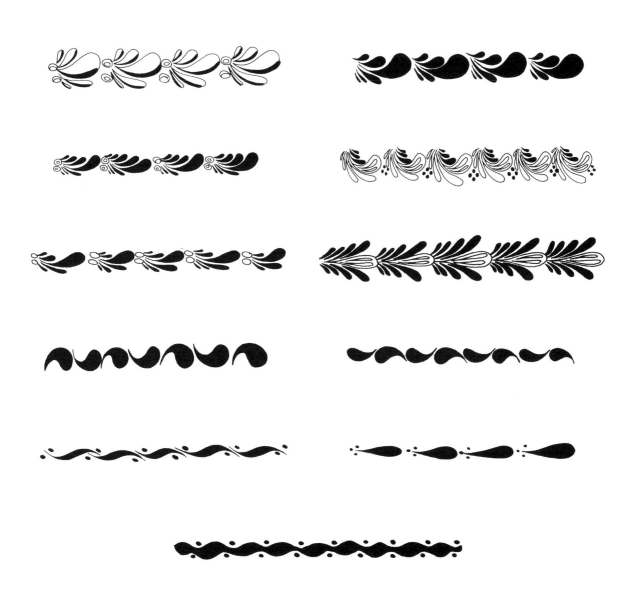

Group I (Mercy North):

Designs Along Base Edge

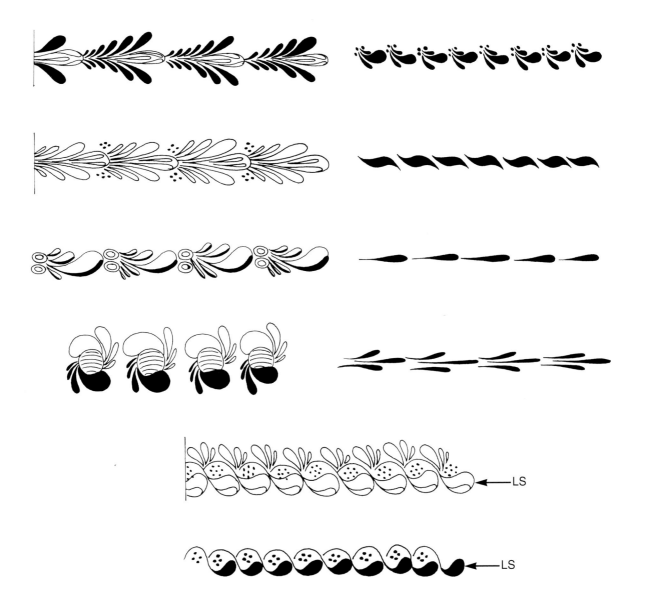

Group I (Mercy North):

8. Lid tops:

a. <u>Brushstroke groupings around the handle painted in red (with alizarin and white overtones), green and yellow. Green strokes may have yellow accent.</u>

b. Brushstroke groups of four (occasionally two) painted in yellow.

c. Outer edge of lid may have "<u>ladle</u>" stroke or brushstroke groups as described under #7a. Most often the edge is plain.

d. No striping.

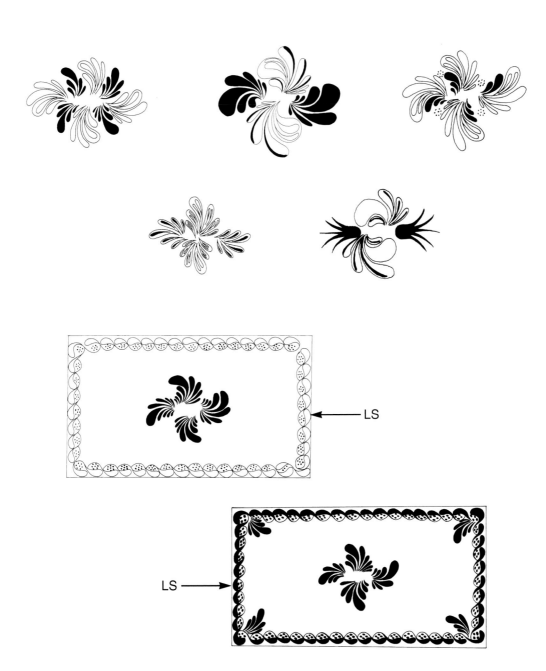

Group I (Mercy North):

9. <u>**Wrap-around designs:**</u> Part of a brushstroke is painted on the front of the trunk while the rest of that same stroke appears on the end. All areas of decoration are treated in this manner including the painted band design, the borders below the band and at the base edge, and the lid front face (on which some strokes may overlap onto the top of the lid).

GROUP II

This group contains designs with painted bands as seen in Group I, although the bands now appear only on the trunk fronts. The "ladle" stroke is often found as a border painted below the banding, or it may appear on the trunk end.

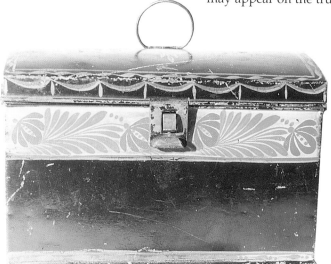

Fig 3.13a, 3.13b and 3.13c. Trunk 9 ⅜" (23.8 cm). Asphaltum. The white band has a painted floral design similar to what has been seen in Group I. A narrow white band at the lower edge shows a simple design. Double striping in red and yellow is used at the edge of the band. Across the front face of the lid is a "swag-and-tassel" border in red and yellow. Fig. 3.13b shows the "ladle" stroke placed horizontally on the end of the lid and diagonally below. This view is of the left end and illustrates that the yellow striping is on the top, back and lower edges. The lid has a stripe and ribbon stroke around the outer edge. The handle is surrounded by brushstrokes painted in a diamond shape.

Collection of Maryjane Clark

Fig. 3.14. Trunk 7 ⅞" (20 cm). Dark asphaltum. This pinkish-red band is adorned with red shells outlined in yellow and green. The "ladle" stroke appears below the band and is found on the trunk end as well. A "swag-and-tassel" border and double striping are also utilized.

Collection of Doris Fry

Fig 3.15. Trunk 4 ½" (11.4 cm). Dark asphaltum. A white band with simple design, swags below and "swag-and-tassel" above are found on this small trunk. It was possibly painted as a gift. On the lower front it says: *Polly Merrill AE 16.*

Collection of Ruth Coggins (deceased)

Fig 3.16a and 3.16b. Trunk 9 ¼" (23.5 cm). Dark asphaltum. The white band, scalloped along the lower edge, contains a vine of flowers and leaflets painted in vivid yellow and an intense deep blue. A narrow white band at the base edge, double striping, and "swag-and-tassel" border are like those previously illustrated. Although it is difficult to discern, the initials *AT* or *ST* are painted below the scalloped band. The lid has only a wide stripe at the outer edge. Surrounding the handle are brushstroke groups arranged in an offset triangular form (see Fig. 3.13c).

Collection of Maryjane Clark

Fig. 3.17. Trunk 9 ⅞" (25.1 cm). Asphaltum. The front of the trunk has an upper band with the added adornment of white circles. Below the band are a narrow band and swags. Green leaves and dark red blossoms with green, yellow and pink overpainting are found on the upper band. Double striping is used at the lower edge of the front face of the lid as well as the base edge.

Private Collection

Fig 3.18. Trunk 8 ⅝" (21.9 cm). Dark asphaltum. This trunk is very similar to that in Fig. 3.16, but has a different treatment at the lower edge of the band. The white "ladle" stroke, outlined with red and yellow, is below the band. The trunk has an inscription scratched inside the lid which reads: *Sam L. Bushells Jr Sheffield April 2, 1818. Bot of a tin peder by the name of Hawley for a paper box. Price one dollar.*

Private Collection

Fig. 3.19. Trunk 9 ¼" (23.2 cm). Dark asphaltum. The shape of the band on this piece is similar to Fig. 3.18. It is overpainted with dark orange motifs outlined in yellow. The remaining decoration is similar to previous pieces.

Collection of Bea Nelson

Fig 3.20. Trunk 8 ⅝" (21.9 cm). Dark asphaltum. Two red bands, each with alternating chevron groups in alizarin and white, are swagged across the front of the trunk. A green stroke outlines the lower edge of the red and there is a narrow red band with alizarin and white dots above. Narrow yellow brushstrokes in graduating sizes extend downward from the red swags. Groups of green brushstrokes with yellow outlines on one side run downward at the left and right sides and under the hasp. Green strokes are also found in the opening above the swagged red bands. The trunk end shows a diagonal yellow rope and three stripes.

Private Collection

Fig. 3.21. Trunk 6 ¼" (15.9 cm). Asphaltum. A red band scalloped at the lower edge is swagged across the entire front. The treatment in the lower corners is interesting. Note that the border across the front face of the lid is similar to borders seen in Group I.

Collection of Cornelia Keegan

Note: Fig. 3.20 and 3.21 exhibit characteristics of Berlin CT painted tinware.
This is not unexpected as Stephen North received his training there.

Group II (Trunks only):

1. Background: asphaltum.

2. Bands (on front only):
    a. Straight bands in white (with red and green motifs), green (with red and yellow motifs) or pink (with red, green, and yellow motifs).
    b. Complex bands in white, often having design-planned openings that allow the background to show through. Floral motifs painted in dark blue and bright yellow, orange and yellow, or dark red and green.
    c. Red band (straight, swagged or scalloped) with alternating groups of alizarin and white strokes. **[B]**
    d. Narrow band with simple dot design may be at base edge and in same color as upper band.
    e. Striping along bands in one or two of the colors used for the motifs.

3. Borders of trunk front:
    a. No designs directly below the band but occasionally a row of small "ladle" strokes may be found.
    b. <u>Front face of lid usually has "swag-and-tassel" design in red and yellow (sometimes with a third color)</u>.

Straight Bands

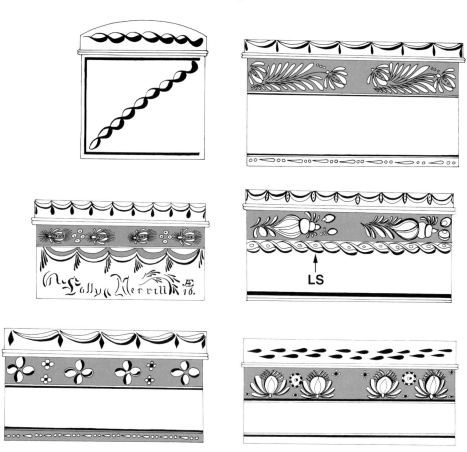

Group II:

Complex Bands

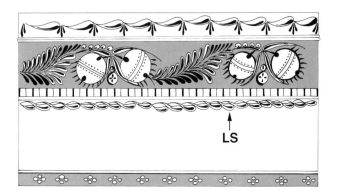

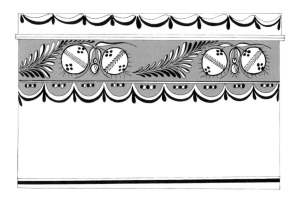

Group II:

Red Bands

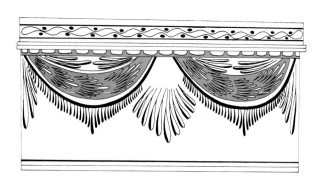 

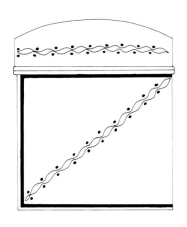 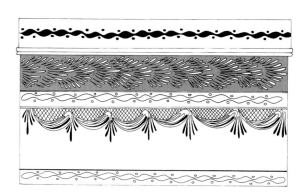

Group II:

4. Lid Tops:

    a. Group of yellow brushstrokes of graduating sizes positioned in front and in back of handle is most commonly found. The strokes of each group are most often curved to the left resulting in an asymmetrical, offset arrangement (occasionally these strokes are straight).

    b. Four groups of yellow and green brushstrokes surround handle.

    c. Yellow stripe (narrow or wide) around outer edge.

    d. Yellow ribbon stroke occasionally.

Group II:

5. Trunk ends:

a. Row of brushstrokes placed diagonally. The left end diagonal will run from the lower back corner of the trunk to the upper front corner. The right end diagonal may run in either direction. Refer to illustrations under Group II: Red Bands.

b. Striping in yellow (narrow or wide) positioned—

    1.) along base edge only

    2.) <u>along base edge, back edge, and top edge</u>

    3.) No stripe along front edge

c. Border on end of lid usually the same strokes as the diagonal or as what appears on the front face of lid.

Trunk End (left)

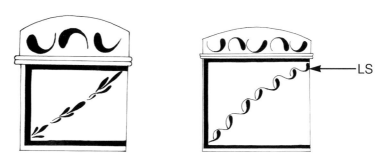

Trunk End (left and right)

GROUP III

This group is comprised of floral spray designs.
The treatment of the trunk ends and lids is very similar to those seen in Group II.

Fig. 3.22. Trunk 6¼" (15.5 cm). Asphaltum. The two large brush-stroke flowers have the same broad center strokes as seen in Group I. Inside the center opening there is a group of small yellow brushstrokes and yellow dots. Extending from the head of these flowers are groups of green and yellow strokes that diminish in size as they approach the sides of the blossom. Red buds appear above the flowers. The border on front face of the lid is the same as in Fig. 3.20.

State Museum of Pennsylvania, Harrisburg, PA

Fig. 3.23. Two–sheet waiter 17¾" x 12" (45 x 30.5 cm). Dark asphaltum. The center flower has a scalloped edge with alizarin and white overtones arranged in a pinwheel formation. Four rose buds and three small flowers are like those described in Fig. 3.22. A wreath of green leaflets surrounds the center flower, each outlined with yellow. Distinct leaves with yellow veins are introduced here, four with long pointed tips and two ovoid forms.

Old Sturbridge Village, Sturbridge, MA

Fig. 3.24. Trunk 9¼" (23.3 cm). Asphaltum. The two central lobed flowers are a new form, but the wreath of leaflets, rose buds, small flowers and painted leaves are like those seen in Fig. 3.23.

Hitchcock Chair Company, Riverton, CT

Fig. 3.25. Trunk 9⅜" (23.8 cm). Asphaltum. The two flowers on each side of the hasp resemble those seen in Fig. 3.24. The rose below the hasp is ovoid and has red petals extending upward. Alizarin details within it form another flower. Circular red buds grow out from the center. New leaf forms are introduced and many have very elongated fine yellow tendrils. The lid front face shows the swag-and-tassel border as seen in Group II.

Anonymous

Fig. 3.26. Trunk 9 ⅜" (23.8 cm). Asphaltum. The flowers, buds and border across the lid are now familiar. New leaf forms are again introduced. They are triangular at their base edge and have yellow lines and dots across the wider edge. Extending from the leaf are three or four extremely long green tendrils with yellow outlines.

Collection of Charlotte Paddock (deceased)

Fig. 3.27. Trunk 8 ½" (21.6 cm). Dark asphaltum. The central rose has the addition of two large petals on each side. The upper extended petals are hidden beneath the brass escutcheon. A group of green brushstrokes with yellow edging is often found at the base of this type of flower. Rose buds are again present and show more detailed painting. An oval leaf, one on each side of the rose, has interesting yellow detail.

Collection of Gina Martin

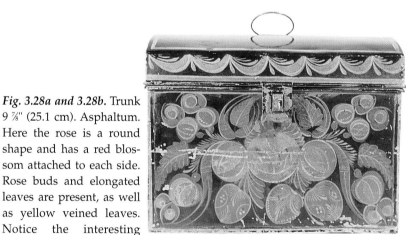

Fig. 3.28a and 3.28b. Trunk 9 ⅞" (25.1 cm). Asphaltum. Here the rose is a round shape and has a red blossom attached to each side. Rose buds and elongated leaves are present, as well as yellow veined leaves. Notice the interesting overpainting on the three leaves at the lower edge. Although a mottled or grained asphaltum background is usually seen only in Group I, this piece exhibits a mottling that resembles tortoiseshell.

Private Collection

Fig. 3.29. Sugar bowl 3 ⅛" (7.9 cm). Asphaltum. The rose and leaf treatment is now familiar. Two additional flower forms are also presented.

Anonymous

Group III (Floral Spray Designs only):

1. Background: asphaltum

2. Flowers and buds: red with alizarin and white overtones.
    a. <u>Petaled flowers with wide center strokes as described in Group I.</u> Flowers
       may have yellow cross hatching, small brushstrokes, or dots in their centers.
    b. Scalloped flowers with pinwheel arranged overtones **[B].**
    c. Roses with extended petals at their upper end. **[B]** A single broad alizarin stroke often painted
       across the lower half of these extended petals **[B]**. Overtones may be painted to create a flower
       within the rose. Rose buds also found.
    d. Circular arrangement of small ball-shapes, sometimes with cross hatching in the center openings.
    e. Round and oval blossoms and buds may have yellow outlining.
    f. Stems are yellow, red, or green.

Group III:

Additional Flower Forms

Note: The top three trunks illustrated above demonstrate a strong influence of Berlin training (refer to Groups I and II under Chapter One.)

Group III:

Roses With Extended Petals (#2.c)

Group III:

3. Leaves:

   a. Groups of straight brushstrokes (one side yellow and one side green, often with yellow accents). Triangular-shaped arrangement with the center stroke the longest and the side strokes gradually diminishing in size. A yellow dot may be placed at base of the center stroke. These groups usually placed at the head of brushstroke flowers. **[B]**

   b. Many green leaf forms–oval, lobed, heart-shaped, elongated. Yellow veins and accents. Larger leaves may have added dots, interior brushstroke groups and/or outlining.
   c. <u>Narrow green leaf with long tendrils extending off the anterior end and long thin yellow accent lines. Two or three yellow lines and dots painted across leaf at area where tendrils begin.</u>
   d. Curved brushstroke groups in yellow and green, or just green. Yellow accents on green strokes.

Additional Leaf Forms

 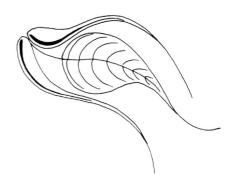

Group III:

4. Borders on front face of lid:

a. <u>"Swag-and-tassel" in red and yellow.</u>
b. Red rick-rack with yellow dots.
c. Groups of brushstrokes with center red stroke and others yellow (or yellow and green). These groups are sometimes separated by red ball-shapes, either singlely or as groups.

Group III:

5. Lid tops:

    a. Treatment at handle the same as Group II. Usually in yellow but may be yellow and green.
       Occasionally four groups of strokes in yellow and green surround the handle.
    b. Stripe around outer edge in yellow (often wide).

Group III:

6. Trunk ends:

    a. Row of brushstrokes placed diagonally as in Group II.

    b. Striping in yellow (narrow or wide) and positioned -

        1.) along base edge only

        2.) <u>along base edge and back edge</u>

        3.) <u>along base edge, back edge, and top edge</u>

        4.) No stripe along front edge

    c. Border strokes on end of lid may be the same as those used in the diagonal or those used on the front face of lid. On occasion an entirely different border is used.

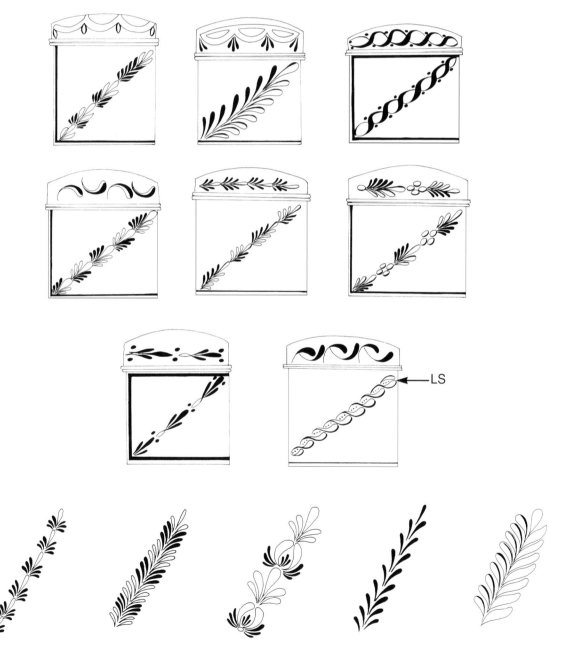

Chapter Four

THE BUTLER TINSHOP
[1824—circa 1855]
East Greenville, New York

Following the Revolutionary War the population of New England grew rapidly. Immigration increased and families remained large despite a high infant mortality. Most original family farms were not large enough to be subdivided to provide a living for the young people as they married and established their own homes. Consequently, land became both scarce and expensive. Many left New England and settled in New York where the original patent owners were beginning to sell off their vast acreage and newly built turnpikes were opening up the area.

In 1799, Abel Butler [1754—1823] and his wife, Mary Brace from West Hartford, left their Connecticut home by oxcart with their seven children —Samuel, Abel, Moses, Aaron, Lydia, Millie, and Hannah. They joined the Yankee invasion, as it was called, and settled in Greenfield, New York, about twelve miles southwest of Albany. Greenfield was organized in 1803 from parts of Coxsackie and Freehold. It had been renamed Freehold in 1808 and again renamed in 1809 to Greenville. The Butlers settled in East Greenville where they purchased a large tract of land with rolling fields and fertile soil. It was a fortunate choice because by 1806, the state legislature approved an act allowing a group of incorporators to establish and maintain the Coxsackie Turnpike which ran past the Butler farm.

The family prospered and in time some of the young people learned a trade, married and moved to neighboring villages. According to the

Historic marker situated on Route 26 in Greenville, New York

Butler Burying Ground at Brandy Hill:

Aaron Butler born March 15, 1790. Died May 12, 1860. Aged 70 yrs, 1 mo., 27 das.

Livingstonville Cemetery marker:

Eli Scutt, born Sept. 20, 1811, died Dec. 22, 1887
Anna M. Butler, his wife, born Aug. 2, 1813, died May 27, 1887
Aaron B. Scutt 1842—1906
H. Adelaide Scutt 1844—1873
M. Frances Scutt 1846—1886

family history, Aaron [1790—1860] was sent to the Berlin Connecticut area to serve as an apprenticeship in tinsmithing, although with whom has not been determined.

It was customary at this period for a young man to start his apprenticeship at about age 15, train for 3 to 5 years, establish his own business the following year, and then marry about a year later. Aaron married Sarah Cornell of Dutchess County in 1811 but did not open his tinshop until 1824 when he was 34. Because of his father's failing health, Aaron apparently became responsible for the family business that included the farm, haypress, cider mill, brandy business and country store. In 1824 after his father's death, Aaron added the tinshop and peddling business to the Brandy Hill enterprises which at times required as many as forty local employees. Aaron became a wealthy and influential man in the town, and at the time of his death, his estate inventory was valued at more than $14,000.

Nine of the eleven children [Ann, Abel, Lewis, Hiram, Marilla, Minerva, Harriet, Aaron Jr., Barnum, Eliza and Sarah Emma] of Aaron and Sarah survived. All attended Greenville Academy, founded in 1816, and then worked for a time for their father. The eldest daughter Ann [1813—1887] learned to paint at an early age, and was most likely taught in all phases of the trade which by 1800 would have included the decorating. She accompanied her father everywhere on his business trips, even to New York City. According to family history, she took charge of the decorating of the tinware at age 14 or 15. It is believed that she, in turn, taught at least Minerva, Marilla and Harriet to paint.

About 1840, Ann's father arranged for her to marry Eli Scutt, a wealthy farmer. She moved to her husband's home in nearby Livingstonville where she raised a family of three children. Marilla Butler [1820—1845] married Ezra Selleck but she died in childbirth at age 25. Minerva Butler [1821—1912] married John Miller from Strausberg, Germany. He was one of Aaron's peddlers, and later managed that part of the Butler business which sent out six to eight peddlers to various parts of the state.

There is no record of the final years of the tinshop; however, Aaron's son, Lewis [1816—1895] carried on the general store during Aaron's last years and took over the farm and store following his father's death. The distillery had been closed around 1859, and the tinshop was closed a few years prior to that. In 1880 he closed the store altogether and continued to work the farm which eventually passed to his granddaughter, Louise, wife of Albert Haight. They added a dance hall and ran it as a resort called Haight's Locust Hill Farm. It was later sold, and then in 1983 was destroyed by fire.

East Greenville mirrored many small villages established in the early days of the Republic. It grew quickly and reached the height of prosperity by 1850. By the turn of the century the old families and businesses were gone, leaving behind only a few buildings in disrepair and overgrown foundations where a bustling community once thrived.

Prepared by Mona D. Rowell and Lois Tucker

BUTLER SHOP: Introduction to the Photographs

It is fortunate that there are many Butler pieces that were signed. There are also many items that have passed down through Butler family members. We have been able to include quite a few of these known Butler pieces in this chapter. So many signed items have been available for study that noting characteristics and painting techniques for this shop has been a relatively easy task.

In the 1930s a group of seven pieces of decorated tinware was released at auction by a branch of the Butler family. Twenty years later these items were given to the Historical Society of Early American Decoration by Katherine Oldham and Anne Bornstraeger in memory of their mother, Mrs. Arthur Oldham. These pieces formed the basis on which the Society's collection was built. Five of these items are included in the photographs [Figs. 4.2, 4.3, 4.4, 4.6, and 4.10 b].

Many years ago and long after the Butler tinshop had closed down, a collection of two hundred bread baskets was discovered in a store room in Greenville. They were decorated with the more simplified designs used on pieces for the trade. For whatever reason, they had never made it to market and were in mint condition. It is still possible for the contemporary collector of tinware today to find one of these bread baskets in antique markets.

Figure captions by Mona D. Rowell and Lois Tucker

Ann Butler

Greenville

Fig. 4.1a, 4.1b and 4.1c. Trunk 10 ⅛" (25.7 cm). Asphaltum. The construction of this large platform-topped trunk with the brass lock shows an English influence. It is signed on the base *Ann Butler, Greenville.* The top of the lid (Fig. 4.1c) is decorated with bouquets of roses and buds, as well as a tulip-type flower with turned back petals. Alizarin and white overtones are used, and white dots are added on top of some of the white strokes as well. Flowers stems are red. Leaves are oval shaped and show a highlight on one side painted in light blue edged by a yellow stroke. Veining is done in black. The platform edge of the lid has an opaque white band with a running vine of leaves and

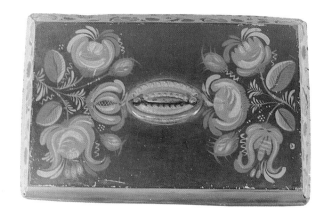

flowers on the upper portion. The lower section of this band has alternating single leaves and pinwheel flowers on the trunk front, and leaves and star-petaled flowers on each end. The front design of this trunk (Fig. 4.1a) shows a single large petaled flower with a spray extending to each side that consists of rosebuds, leaves, and a three-lobed strawberry. The trunk end (Fig.4.1b) displays a spray of rosebuds, while the other end (not shown) has a floral spray similar to those on the lid. Yellow zig-zags and dot clusters are used profusely as space fillers.

Collection of Charlotte Paddock (deceased)

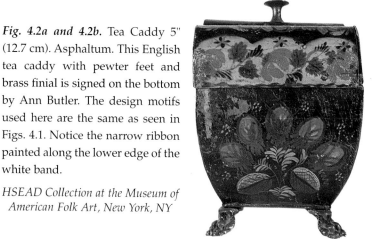

Fig. 4.2a and 4.2b. Tea Caddy 5" (12.7 cm). Asphaltum. This English tea caddy with pewter feet and brass finial is signed on the bottom by Ann Butler. The design motifs used here are the same as seen in Figs. 4.1. Notice the narrow ribbon painted along the lower edge of the white band.

HSEAD Collection at the Museum of American Folk Art, New York, NY

Fig 4.3. Tea Canister 8" (20.3 cm). Asphaltum. Another piece that is signed *Ann Butler, Greenville*. The main design is similar to Figs. 4.1 and 4.2. The white band is scalloped along its lower edge, and the edge is enhanced by yellow painted dots and dashes. Black crosshatching appears in the openings of the flowers.

HSEAD Collection at the Museum of American Folk Art, New York, NY

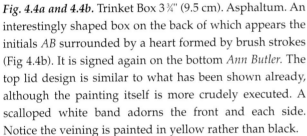

Fig. 4.4a and 4.4b. Trinket Box 3 ¾" (9.5 cm). Asphaltum. An interestingly shaped box on the back of which appears the initials *AB* surrounded by a heart formed by brush strokes (Fig 4.4b). It is signed again on the bottom *Ann Butler*. The top lid design is similar to what has been shown already, although the painting itself is more crudely executed. A scalloped white band adorns the front and each side. Notice the veining is painted in yellow rather than black.

HSEAD Collection at the Museum of American Folk Art, New York, NY

Fig. 4.5a and 4.5b. Box 4" (10.1 cm). Asphaltum. An unusual box which may have been used as a bank. Notice the slot cut into the side in Fig. 4.5b. Signed *Ann Butler* on the bottom, it depicts the same motifs as previously seen.

Collection of Charlotte Paddock (deceased)

Fig. 4.6a and 4.6b. Trunk 6 ¾" (17.1 cm). Asphaltum. This dome-topped trunk exhibits a nearly identical design to Fig. 4.1. The white band is painted around the outside of the lid, and continues over the edge to the front face and upper curve of each end. The end is decorated by yellow brush strokes in a six-petal arrangement with each petal having short thorny extensions along its sides. This piece is also signed on the back *AB* in a heart.

HSEAD Collection at the Museum of American Folk Art, New York, NY

Fig. 4.7. Trunk 7 ⅝" (19.4 cm). Asphaltum. This trunk is adorned with a colorful basket of red, blue, yellow, green, and white. The floral sprays are the same as already seen. The elongated leaves on the front face of the lid are smooth-edged while those on the top lid are serrated. The trunk end shows groups of yellow brushstrokes with a red center strokes. It is signed on the back *AB* in a heart.

Collection of Charlotte Paddock (deceased)

Fig. 4.8. Painting on Paper 11 ⅝" x 13 ⅝" (29.5 x 34.6 cm). Although this framed paper painting is unsigned, it seems likely to have been done by Ann as it demonstrates the types of units seen on her signed pieces.

Anonymous

Fig. 4.9a and 4.9b. Trunk 9 ⅝" (24.4 cm). Asphaltum. This trunk illustrates motifs indistinguishable from those we have already seen; however, the bottom is signed in black paint *Minerva Butler.* That Ann probably trained her siblings to paint would seem quite obvious after studying this piece. Excepting that the painting is not executed as well as Ann's pieces, there are few differences. The yellow border painted on the inner edge of the white band of the lid is different, as is the use of blue surrounding the red dots on the trunk end units.

Collection of Charlotte Paddock (deceased)

Fig. 4.10a and 4.10b. Trunk 4 ⅛" (10.5 cm). Black and Red Backgrounds. These small trunks exhibit white band designs that are very similar. The black trunk is signed on the back with yellow paint *MB* in a heart. The *AB* signature on the red trunk is illustrated in Fig. 4.10b. The hearts on each piece are painted identically. The red is a most unusual background color for this tinshop. It is unfortunate that this important piece of tinware was stolen some years ago from an HSEAD display at the Farmer's Museum in Cooperstown, NY.

Collection of Charlotte Paddock (deceased) and Unknown

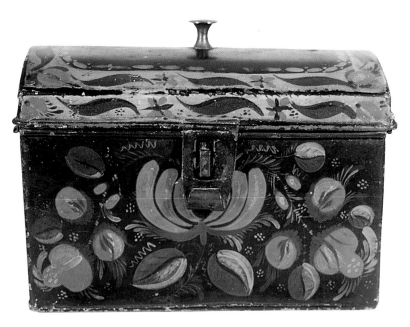

Fig. 4.11. Bread basket 13" (33 cm). Asphaltum. This elaborately decorated piece, owned by Butler family descendants, is signed on the bottom *HB*, which probably stands for Harriet Butler. There is more blue color used on this piece, including the star-flowers, the brush strokes around the large red flowers, small ribbon along the outer edge of the white band, and even the design on the floor has blue brush strokes throughout. The floral spray under the scalloped white band on the ends is similar to other already discussed.

Collection of Beatrice Terhune

Fig. 4.12. Bread basket 13" (33 cm). Asphaltum. According to family tradition, this piece was decorated by Hiram Butler (1818—1851). He had been crippled from a schoolyard accident and was always confined by his infirmity. He learned to paint and to do beadwork. The simple vine on the white bands exhibits units that show influence of Connecticut training, such as solid red flowers and red berries. The lower edge of the scalloped band has a green stroke along its side. The use of the narrow yellow band with the wavy black line through its center is most often found on pieces from Connecticut.

Collection of Charlotte Paddock (deceased)

Fig. 4.13. Trunk 6 ⅝" (16.8 cm). Black. This trunk is signed on the back in yellow paint *SN* within a brush-stroke heart. This painter is not yet identified. The design is again nearly identical to those previously seen, although more crudely executed. Note the brass finial on the lid.

Collection of Beatrice Terhune

Fig. 4.14. Trunk 9⅝" (24.4 cm). Black. This trunk has descended through the family of Harriet Butler Miller. It depicts the same style of flowers but the entire design, as well as the yellow border painting, is much more simplified.

Collection of Charlotte Paddock (deceased)

Fig. 4.15. Trunk 9¼" (23.2 cm). Asphaltum. The floral spray is familiar. Oval leaves of a bright green have yellow veining. Brush stroke groupings adorn each end and also the top of the lid.

Coffin Collection at the National Museum of American History, Washington, DC

Fig. 4.16. Trunk 9½" (24.1 cm). Asphaltum. The yellow outlining of the leaves is a new feature.

Anonymous

Fig. 4.17. Canister 8⅞" (22.5 cm). Black. This canister shows a large central flower with hearts formed by white dots. Notice the lack of pigmentation in the yellow brush strokes.

Collection of Charlotte Paddock (deceased)

Fig. 4.18. Trunk 8 ½" (21.6 cm). Black. White overtones on the red flowers clearly show a heavy white stroke that accents the outer curve of a thinner applied white stroke. This technique of double layers of white overpainting is often seen on Butler pieces. Notice also the row of white dots on the right-hand flower. This is the same treatment seen on Ann's pieces in Fig. 4.1, 4.2, and 4.3. The end of the trunk has a brush stroke grouping done in two colors.

Collection of Doris Fry

Fig. 4.19a and 4.19b. Tea canister 5" tall (12.7 cm). Asphaltum. This one-pound canister shows the simple four-petaled flower motif on one side, and a large red circular flower on the opposite side. Alizarin and white are used for overtones.

Anonymous

Fig. 4.20. Tea canister 5" tall (12.7 cm). Asphaltum. The four-point star design on the canister is suggestive of those seen on the white bands in previous illustrations, as well as the star arrangements used on trunk ends. Green and yellow strokes, and yellow dots surround the red. The reverse side of this canister shows the same circular flower as Fig. 4.19b.

Collection of Beatrice Terhune

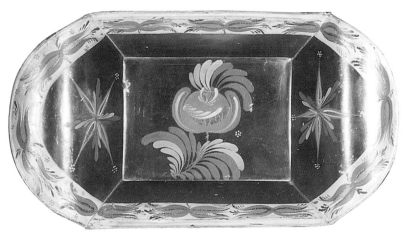

Fig. 4.21. Bread basket 13" (33 cm). Asphaltum. This rectangular bread basket is elaborately decorated. The red and green units on the white band resemble elongated rose buds. A single rose is on the floor, and the four-petaled star appears on each end.

Collection of Beatrice Terhune

Fig. 4.22. Bread basket 12 ¾" (32.4 cm). Black. This oval bread basket with hand holes is signed *MB* on the bottom. The central flower now has six petals and a profusion of interior yellow dots. Although striping is rarely seen on Butler pieces, the upper border here has one along with the large "S" strokes.

HSEAD Collection at the Museum of American Folk Art, New York, NY

Fig. 4.23. Bread basket 12 ¼" (31.1 cm). Black. This oval basket is also signed *MB* and again shows the four-petal star design. Notice the interesting brush stroke and dot border atop a yellow stripe.

Collection of O. C. Stevens

Fig. 4.24. Bread basket 12 ½" (31.1 cm). Black. A spray of three rose buds and a simple ribbon border adorn this oval bread basket.   *Collection of Beatrice Terhune*

Fig. 4.25. Bread basket 12 ¾" (32.4 cm). Black. Seen again is the flower with elongated curving side petals, and now with interior dots. The same border as Fig. 4.22 and quite possibly by the same hand.

Collection of O. C. Stevens

Fig. 4.26. Bread basket 12 ¾" (32.4 cm). Black. This floral spray is familiar but the central flower is a new form. The border is a yellow ribbon with dots.

Collection of Charlotte Paddock (deceased)

Fig 4.27. Bread basket 9 ¾" (24.8 cm). Black. The round flower on the floor of this oval bread basket is similar to those already shown, but it is without any side petals. Alizarin and white overtones are used. Groups of ovoid leaves with yellow veins surround the flower.

Collection of Charlotte Paddock (deceased)

Fig. 4.28. Bread basket 12 ½" (31.8 cm). Black. This oval basket has pierced sides which is a rare form.

Collection of Charlotte Paddock (deceased)

Fig. 4.29. Bread basket 13 ½" (34.3 cm). Black. The flower has six petals here and the leaves each have a wide yellow outline.

Collection of O. C. Stevens

Fig. 4.30. Bread basket 12 ¼" (30.8 cm). Black. A similar design once more although the leaves here are elongated and curved.

Collection of O. C. Stevens

Fig. 4.31. Bread basket 13 ⅝" (34.6 cm). Black. The rose is similar to others we've seen but now shows a central opening that contains three yellow brush strokes.

HSEAD Collection at the Museum of American Folk Art, New York, NY

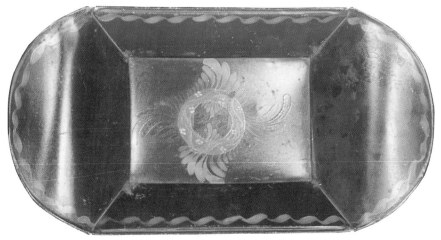

Fig. 4.32. Bread basket 13 ¾" (34.9 cm). Black. An unusual red circle with alizarin and white overpainting. Groups of yellow and green leaflets are arranged in a similar manner to other designs seen throughout.

Collection of Liz Bach

CHARACTERISTICS OF BUTLER SHOP DECORATION

The drawn illustrations will show the characteristics in greater detail than the photographs. The letters that accompany each drawing identify the painter of the piece as follows: AB=Ann Butler; MB=Minerva Butler; HB=Harriet Butler; SN=unknown; EL=unknown; X=unsigned.

Colors found on Butler pieces:

Red—vermilion

Green—medium, dark and olive

Yellow—chrome medium (occasionally very thin)

White—opaque for bands, thin for overtones

Alizarin—thin for overtones

Blue—medium, light blue used as leaf highlights

Black—used for detail and space fillers

Types of decorated tinware found:

Trunks (dome-topped) in various sizes—Large trunks decorated for the trade are often found to be not as deep as usually expected. The measurements of the trunk end (its length and height) are nearly identical. This gives the trunk a short squatty appearance.

Bread baskets—rectangular (both deep and shallow), oval with or without handholes, oval with pierced sides (Rare!)

Tea canisters—round and oval

Canister—large round size

Fancy tinware pieces—English tea caddy, trinket boxes, ball-footed trunk

Illustrations selected by Gina Martin and Lois Tucker
Line drawings by Gina Martin and Lois Tucker

AB

Refer to page xv for the guide to interpretation of the line drawings.

1. **Backgrounds:** Asphaltum used on pieces with white bands (one has a red background) and commercial pieces are black.

2. **White Bands:** Usually straight edged but occasionally a scalloped edge. <u>The band on the end of a trunk will be curved to follow the upper edge of the lid.</u> The bands were used on fancy pieces made for special relatives or friends, but not for the general trade.

3. **Flowers:**

    a. Painted in red. Sometimes blue was also incorporated.

    b. Roses and buds, tulips with curved back outer petals, 3-lobed "strawberry" flower, star-shaped flowers, and 4 or 6-petaled brushstroke flowers.

    c. Stems painted red (occasionally green). Often have two yellow hash marks.

    d. Overtones done in white and alizarin. White often in two layers, such as a small stroke alongside a larger one, <u>and dots added through the center of the brushstroke.</u>

    e. Green petals at base of largest flowers - especially on the fancier pieces.

    f. Rose buds have green tendrils that cross over the bud and extend beyond.

    g. Flower openings may have crosshatching (in single or double lines) and dots.

    h. Star-shaped flowers painted in two colors.

    i. Blue colors used on the fancy pieces.

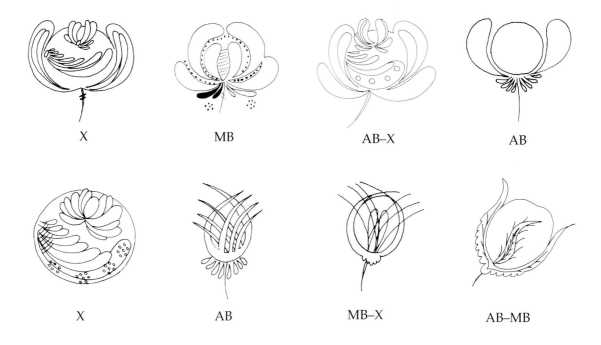

    X   MB   AB–X   AB

    X   AB   MB–X   AB–MB

Flowers

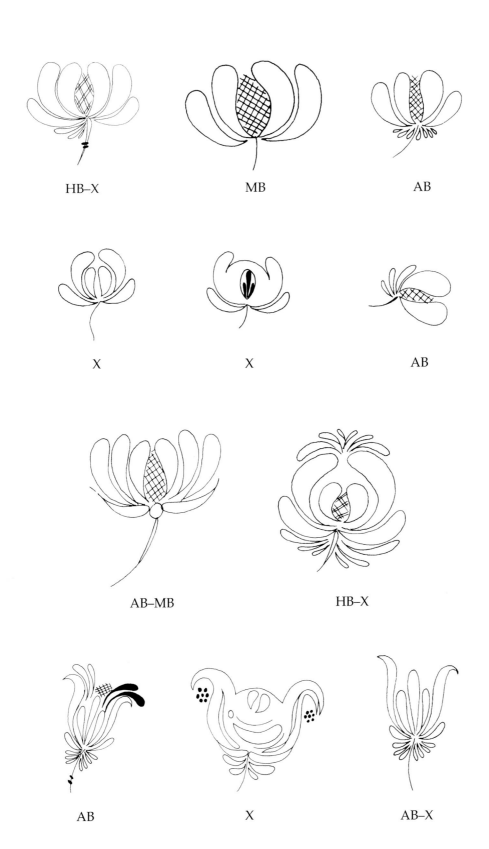

HB–X

MB

AB

X

X

AB

AB–MB

HB–X

AB

X

AB–X

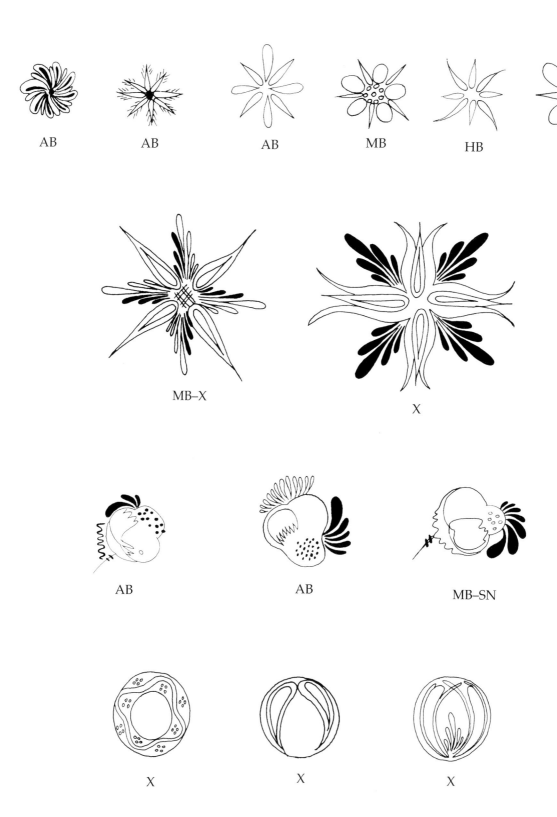

AB   AB   AB   MB   HB   SN

MB–X

X

AB   AB   MB–SN

X   X   X

4. Leaves:

a. Large leaves may be oval or pointed.

b. Elongated leaves with smooth or serrated edges used on white bands.

c. Veining black on white bands and may extend beyond the edge of the leaf. Veining in black or yellow elsewhere.

d. <u>Large leaves may have a highlight of light blue edged with yellow.</u>

e. Leaves may have a yellow outline all around.

f. Brushstroke leaflets in green and yellow groups placed along a stem.

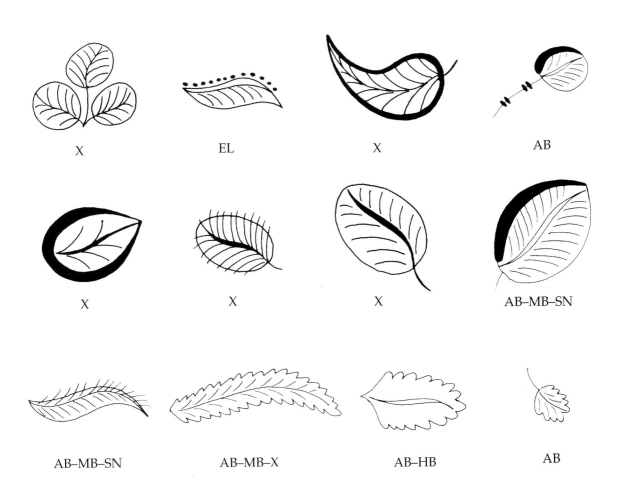

| X | EL | X | AB |

| X | X | X | AB–MB–SN |

| AB–MB–SN | AB–MB–X | AB–HB | AB |

5. Additional Embellishments:

    a. Yellow hash-lines across stems (either straight or curved).

    b. Dot-flowers used profusely on fancy pieces (in red, black, yellow, green, or blue).

    c. Zig-zagged lines used as space fillers.

AB   Used by all   AB–MB–SN

6. Brushstroke Borders:

    a. Ribbon or rick rack (with or without added dots). White bands may be edged with very tiny rick rack strokes in black or blue.

    b. Rope, sometimes with a stripe through center.

    c. Groups of brushstrokes on trunk end, sometimes very long strokes.

    d. Short straight sausage-shaped strokes separated by two dots.

    e. Borders painted in yellow, and occasionally a red stroke is used in the center of a group.

7. Striping: Not commonly found

Trunk Lids with White Bands

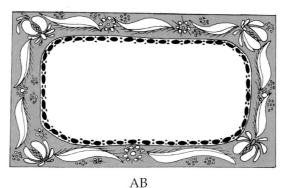

AB

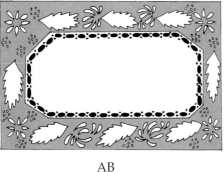

AB

AB

Trunk Lids with White Bands

MB   X

Trunk Lids (no bands)

All lids above are from unsigned pieces.

Trunk Ends with White Bands

AB

AB

X

AB

EL

Trunk Ends

AB

SN

MB

Trunk Ends

All trunk ends above are from unsigned pieces.

Brushstroke Borders

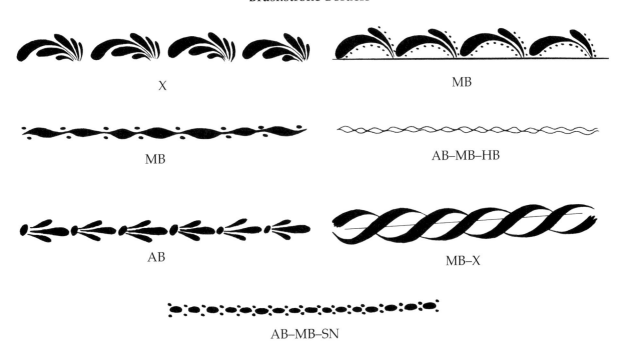

APPENDIX A

CHECKLIST FOR TINSHOP IDENTIFICATION: This checklist has been designed solely for the purpose of leading the identifying process in the proper direction. An unknown piece of japanned ware can be inspected to determine the basic elements of its characteristics. These in turn should be located on the checklist to discover which shop may have been the manufacturer. By then turning to the section of this book that deals with that particular tinshop, the reader should be able to confirm the identity after studying the photograph and drawing sections. It may require checking several shops before a final determination can be made as certain characteristics were used by more than one shop. An expanded checklist will be included in future volumes in order to add those additional shops, along with their distinctive characteristics, to this checklist.

		BERLIN	UPSON	NORTH	BUTLER
Background	Asphaltum	X	X	X	X
	Asphaltum (mottled)			X	
	Black	X			X
	Crystalizing		X		
	Red	X	X		X
	Other colors		X		
Painted Bands	White	X	X	X	X
	Red	X		X	
	Blue	X			
	Green	X		X	
	Pink			X	
	Yellow (¼" wide)		X		
	Straight	X	X	X	X
	Scalloped	X	X	X	X
	Swagged	X	X	X	
	Unusual shapes and complicated forms	X	X	X	
	Green swag alongside a red swag	X			
Flower Forms	Roses with extended upper petals	X		X	
	Lobular-shaped blossoms	X			
	Heart-shaped blossoms	X			
	Groups of four round buds	X			
	Scallop-edged flowers	X	X	X	
	Open centers		X		
	Morning glories		X		
	Single stroke petals with center petals very large			X	
	Tulips with curved back petals				X
	Star-shaped flowers				X
	Stamens within flower centers		X		
Stems (Flower)	Red	X		X	X

		BERLIN	UPSON	NORTH	BUTLER
Fruits	Peaches		X		
	Grapes		X		
	Cherries		X		
	Pears		X		
	Strawberries				X
Misc. Motifs	Shells		X	X	
	Basket				X
Overtones	'Cobra' stroke	X			
	Alizarin painted over one-half of bud	X			
	Pinwheel-shape	X		X	
	Ribbon stroke	X			
	Crescent-shaped (narrow)	X			
	Crosswise-to-flower positioning	X			
	Large swag across whole flower	X			
	Chevron groupings	X		X	
	Dark blue on white band			X	
	Candy-stripe arrangement	X		X	
	Fingered-off technique		X		
	White overtones in two layers				X
	White stroke with white dots inside				X
	Scallop-edged		X		
Leaves	Round or oval	X	X	X	X
	Pointed	X	X	X	X
	Serrated	X	X		X
	Three-lobed		X		
	Elongated forms			X	X
	Turned-over tips		X		
	Split center opening		X		
	Yellow accents or outlining	X		X	X
	Blue highlight				X
	Narrow with long tendrils			X	
	Veining in black		X		X
	Cross veins as curved lines		X		
Accents	'Signature' squiggles		X		
	Undulating squiggles	X			
	Curlicues along stem lines	X			
	Dots and dot circles			X	X
	Zig zags				X
	Hash lines on stems				X
	Cross-hatching in double lines	X			X
	Green accents on white units		X		
Trunk Ends	Single round flower and leaflets	X			
	Floral spray	X		X	X
	Horizontal rows of border strokes	X			
	Diagonal row of strokes	X		X	
	Scalloped yellow line with teardrops	X	X		
	"Swag-and-tassel" arrangement			X	
	Painted band on uppermost edge				X
	Ribbon stroke - compact and tightly formed	X			
	Ribbon stroke along all edges of trunk	X			
	Ribbon stroke forming large X	X			
	Four round units and leaflets	X			

		BERLIN	UPSON	NORTH	BUTLER
Trunk Lids	Wide stripe around outer edge			X	
	Four or more groupings around handle			X	
	Multicolored groupings around handle			X	
	Brushstroke cluster flowers along stripe lines		X		
	Asymmetrical groupings at handle			X	
	Ribbon stroke in blue	X			
	Narrow red band around edge	X			
Borders	Lattice fence (with or without dots)	X		X	
	White berries with yellow brushstroke groups	X			
	Red berries with green or red brushstroke groups			X	
	Two or more colors used	X	X	X	
	Green ribbon	X			
	Red ribbon			X	
	No border on front lid face	X			
Striping	Red stripe along white band		X	X	
	Double striping	X	X		
	Along two or three edge of trunk ends			X	
	Wide stripe around edge of trunk lid			X	
	Not commonly found				X
Designs	Geometrically balanced	X			
	Wrap-around			X	
Unusual Technique	Semi-impasto	X			

APPENDIX B

The following is a copy of the agreement among the Berlin tinners for setting the minimum prices for their tinware. The prices are listed in shillings and pence, the common monetary units of the period. The document lists all the tinware pieces manufactured by these tinners. The listing does not imply that every man produced each different piece in his shop; however, the list does provide us with an accounting of all the various items that were manufactured and decorated in the Berlin area tinshops.

"WE THE SUBSCRIBERS each and every one of us agree not to sell off tinware plain and japanned below the prices apprised to the several articles...June 16, 1813.

Signed: Shubael Pattison, Orin Beckley, Samuel Pattison, John Dunham, Samuel Gilbert, John Goodrich Sr., Aziel Belden, John Buckman, John Hubbard, Benjamin Wilcox, Samuel Kelsey, and Patrick Clark."

JAPANNED TINWARE

Large Trunks .5/	Quart Measures (*Mugs*) /10
2nd Size Trunks .4/6	Spring Candlestick /10
3rd Size Trunks .3/	Sugar Bowls /10
4th Size Trunks .2/6	Molasses Cups (*Syrup Pitcher*) /10
Large Size Sugar Boxes (*Round Canisters*) .4/	Half Sheet Waiters /9
2nd Size Sugar Boxes .3/	Back Candlesticks (*Sconces*) /9
3rd Size Sugar Boxes .2/4	Large Raised Bottom Candlesticks /9
4th Size Sugar Boxes .1/6	Half Pound Canister /9
Crooked Spout Coffee Pots .3/	Milk Cups (*Creamers*) /6
Two Sheet Waiters (*Trays*) .4/	Quarter Pound Canisters /6
Three Quart Coffee Pots .2/4	Pint Measures /6
Knife Trays .2/4	Flour Boxes (*Dredgers*) /6
Large Eight Square Bread Pans .2/	Pint Tumblers /5
Large Bread Pans .1/6	Small Raised Bottom Spring Candlesticks /5
Three Pint Coffee Pots .1/6	Comb Cases /5
Large Teapots .1/6	Sugar Boxes /5
Small Eight Square Bread Pans .1/6	Half Pint Tumblers /5
Small Teapots .1/1	Gill Tumblers /3 ½
Small Bread Pans .1/1	Kneedle Cases /3 ½
Sheet Waiters .1/1	Pepper Boxes (*Pepper Shakers*) /3 ½
Raised Bottom Spring Candlesticks .1/1	Snuffer Trays /3½
Pound Canisters (*Tea Canisters*) .1/1	Sand Boxes (*Sand Shakers*) /3 ½
	Small Back Candlesticks /2 ½
	Extinguishers (*Douters*) /2

PLAIN TINWARE

Large Ovens	2 Size Oven
	3 Size Oven
	4 Size Oven

Large Dish Kettles 5/6
Water Pots 4/6
Large Pails 4/
Large Pans 4/
Stoves 4/
Ten quart pans 3/4
Ten quart pails 3/4
Gallon Coffee Pot 3/4
Large Coverd Pails 3/4
Large Sauce Pans 3/4
Gallon Measures 2/4
Six quart pails 2/4
Common size milk pans 2/4
Large wash bowles 2/4
Lanterns 2/4
Small dish kettles 2/4
Cullinders 2/4
Three quart coffee pots 2/4
Large pudding baggs .2/4
Roasters 2/4
Lantern pans 2/
Two quart Coffee pots 2/
Three quart Covered pails 2/
Small wash bowles 2/
Small sauce pans 2/
Half gallon measures .1/6
Half gallon pans 1/6
Half gallon dippers 1/6
Half gallon funnels 1/6
Three pint Coffee pot .1/6
Small covered pails 1/6
Large blow horns 1/6
Three quart pails 1/6
Round pans 1/1
Large square pans 1/1
Large scallop pans 1/1
Sausage Horns 1/1
Quart Coffee pots 1/1
Square toast pans 1/1
Small pails 1/1

Round flat bottom Teapots 1/1
Second size horns 1/1
Sailor pots 1/1
Lamp fillers 1/1
Water Ladles 1/1
Sugar scoops 1/1
Milk strainers 1/1
Quart measures . . . ./10
Large skimmers . . . ./10
Quart funnels . . . ./10
Small horns . . . ./10
Saisons . . . ./9
Quart scallops . . . ./9
Quart sauce pans . . . ./9
Round handled dipper . . . ./9
Half Sheet square pans . . . ./7
Half Sheet funnels . . . ./7
Half Sheet dippers . . . ./7
Half Sheet scallops . . . ./7
Half Sheet graters . . . ./7
Pint measures . . . ./6
Pint cups . . . ./6
Pint graters . . . ./6
Pint scallops . . . ./6
Pint candlemolds . . . ./6
Flour boxes . . . ./6
Half pint measure . . . ./3 ½
Half pint cups . . . ./3 ½
Half pint dippers . . . ./3 ½
Gill measures . . . ./3 ½
Half pint funnels . . . ./3 ½
Baisters . . . ./3 ½
Small skimmers . . . ./3 ½
Flat candlesticks . . . ./3 ½
Small candlemolds . . . ./3 ½
Kneedle cases . . . ./3 ½
Pepper boxes . . . ./3 ½
Hearts *(Cookie Cutters)* . . . ./2
Rounds *(Cookie Cutters)* . . . ./2
Ratt Boxes . . . ./2
Small graters . . . ./2
Whistles

APPENDIX C

MERCHANDISE SOLD AT PATTISON & PECK STORE for period 1815 to 1818
as listed in the account journal of Elisha Peck.

Common tinplate	Pork	Muslin	Alum
Thick tin	Beef	Stockinett	Chalk
Damaged tin	Codfish	Velvet	Nicaraugan wood
Sodder	Chickens	Millinett	Walnut wood
Iron wire in various sizes	Oysters	Coating	Door handles
Copper	Flour–wheat and rye	Twist	Locks
Old pewter	Rice	Gingham	Files
Brass	Oats	Silk	Awl blades
Iron	Sugar–lump and brown	Vesting	Shingles
Rivets	Tea, coffee, and coffee mills	Ribbon	Brass knobs
	Maple sugar	Cambric	Tacks
Gun powder	Molasses	Cashmere	Nails–iron and brass
Flints	Potatoes	Linen	Screws
Shot	Crackers	Bombagett	Window glass
	Raisins	India calico	
Candles	Butter	Cotton shirting	Silverware
Beeswax	Cheese	Flannel	Stoneware and crockery
Tallow	Eggs	Flax	Chinaware
Wick yarn	Salt	Wool	
Tar	Corn	Yarn	Postage stamps
	Fruit	Thread	Writing paper
Fire dogs	Peppermint	Needles	Spelling books
Wrapping paper	Wintergreen	Thimbles	
	Chocolate	Scissors	Shawls
Cotton roll	Cloves	Buttons and button molds	Hose
Feathers	Nutmeg	Gimblets	Bonnets and hats
Blankets	Pepper		Gloves–silk and kid
Pillows	Ginger	Rosin (by the barrel)	Cravat and stickpins
	Cinnamon	Turpentine	Handkerchief
Carpeting & binding		Lamp black	Moracco shoes
Hogsheads	Rum	White lead	Boots
	Brandy	Chrome yellow	Shoe knife
Castor oil	Lisbon wine	and patent yellow	
Opium	Gin	Chinese vermilion	Combs (horn) - side combs
Snuff and tobacco	Cider		and fan top
Gum camphor		Paint brushes	
Elixir asthmatic	Soap		
Ether vitrol	Shaving boxes		

APPENDIX D

TYPES OF TINWARE manufactured by R. & B. Wilcox of Middletown, CT
as related in the correspondences between 1817 and 1831.

Japanned Ware:

Trunks in various sizes
Teapots, large and small
Waiters– ½-sheet, 1-sheet, and 2-sheet
Tumblers– ½-pint and pint
Bread pans– large and small; oval, square
Candlestick with spring
Candlestick– ½-sheet
B. candlestick
Sugar bowls

Sugar boxes in various sizes
Pound canisters
Molasses cup
Pepper boxes
Needle cases
Snuffer tray
Comb cases
Knife trays

Plain Tinware:

Wash basins
Lantern– large and small
Basin ladles

APPENDIX E

TINWARE ARTICLES dispensed by John Hubbard as listed in his account books from 1818 to 1822.

Japanned Tin:

Large bread baskets
Small bread baskets
Oval bread baskets
½-pound canisters
½-sheet and 1-sheet waiters
Sugar bowls
Teapots, large and small
Large servers
Pound canister
Extinguishers

Flour boxes
Pepper boxes
Large trunk
Nest trunks
Pints and quarts
½-pints
Square bread pans
Fruit basket
Molasses cup

Plain Tin:

Dish kettles
Milk pans
Lantern pans
Round pans
Quart pans
½-sheets
Dippers
Pint scalloped pans
Rattles
Collanders
Water pots
Teapots
Lanterns

Large pails
Covered pails
Wash bowls
½-gallons
Quarts
½-pints
Small oven
Middling size oven
Large oven
Small grater
Pint cups
Large coffee pots
Whistles

APPENDIX F

BERLIN AREA TINNERS AND PEDDLERS as gleaned from account books, day books, letters, genealogical sources, newspapers, census records, and land records researched for this publication.

Andrews, Asa. (1769—1831) Farmington tinner whose shop was at the fork of the road and just south of the meeting house. Apprentice Solomon Carrington, who had an amputated leg, was bound to him in August 1805 to learn the trade of japanning tinplate. Apprentice Allen Robinson was bound to him in May 1816 to learn the trade of japanning tin work. Listed in the town assessment list for 1797 and 1798 as a tinner.

Andrews, Jesse. Mentioned in Jedediah North's account books of 1820 to 1822.

Andrews, Silas. Mentioned in Jedediah North's account books of 1820 to 1822.

Bacon, Joel. Mentioned in Jedediah North's account books of 1820 to 1822.

Bacon, Nathaniel. Mentioned in Jedediah North's account books of 1820 to 1822 and John Hubbard's account books.

Bailey, Mr. Peddled for R & B Wilcox in the South.

Barber, Silas. Bought tinplate from Pattison & Peck.

Barnes, Blakesley B. Berlin tinner who bought tin plate from Pattison & Peck and tools from J & E North Co.

Barns, Moses. Meriden tinner who died in 1816. Bought tinplate from Pattison & Peck.

Beckley, Chester, Orrin, and Nathaniel. Wethersfield tinners. Brothers who moved to Wilmington, Delaware and established a tin business about 1812.

Beckley, Orin. (1784—1836) Son-in-law of Shubael Pattison and his business associate.

Beckley, Reuben. (b. 1791) Berlin tinner.

Beckley, William. (1803—1832) Wethersfield tinner who eventually went to Wilmington where his cousins ran a tin business.

Belden, Aziel. (b. 1770) Berlin tinner who signed the 1813 pricing agreement.

Belden, Horace. Mentioned in John Hubbard's account books.

Boardman, Nathan. Mentioned in Jedediah North's account books of 1820 to 1822.

Booth, Walter. Meriden tinner. Mentioned in Jedediah North's account books of 1820 to 1822.

Bowers, Harley. (b. 1793) Peddled for R & B Wilcox in the South.

Brook, Stephen. Peddled for R & B Wilcox in the South.

Brown, William F. Mentioned in Jedediah North's account books of 1820 to 1822.

Brunson, Ira. Mentioned in Jedediah North's account books of 1820 to 1822.

Brunson, Samuel. Berlin tinner mentioned in the Peck account books.

Buckley, Moses. Mentioned in the Peck account books.

Bulkley, Col. William. (1797—1878) Berlin tinner and manufacturer of tinmen's tools.

Buckman, John. Berlin tinner who signed the 1813 pricing agreement. Bought tinplate from Pattison & Peck.

Bulkeley & Inman. Berlin makers of tinner's tools mentioned in 1895 Berlin News article *Recollections of Berlin.*

Burham, John. Peddled for Benjamin Wilcox. In a letter to Benjamin he says he has also peddled for Mr. Lord in Windsor, VT.

Burrows, Asahel. Berlin peddler.

Butler, John. Mentioned in Jedediah North's account books of 1820 to 1822.

Cannon, Lyman. Wallingford tinner. Processed 50 boxes of tinplate in 1820.

Carrion & Goodrich. Bought tinplate from Pattison & Peck.

Carter, Gad. Mentioned in Jedediah North's account books of 1820 to 1822.

Cheney, Elisha. Mentioned in Jedediah North's account books of 1820 to 1822.

Church, John. Mentioned in Jedediah North's account books of 1820 to 1822.

Clark, Patrick. Meriden tinner.

Clark, Revlo. Mentioned in Jedediah North's account books of 1820 to 1822.

Clark, Samuel. Peddled for R & B Wilcox in the South.

Collins, Edward. Meriden tinner.

Cook, Dennis. Mentioned in Jedediah North's account books of 1820 to 1822.

Cowles, Elisha A. Bought tinplate from Pattison & Peck.

Cramton, William. Peddled for R & B Wilcox in the South.

Crittenden, Norman. Employed by J & E North Co.

Crittenden, Nathaniel. Peddler for John Hubbard.

Crofoot, Joseph. Mentioned in John Hubbard's account books.

Curtis, Emery. Mentioned in John Hubbard's account books.

Curtis, Thomas S. Bought tinplate from Pattison & Peck.

Danforth, Thomas. Wethersfield tinner to whom Ashbel Russel was apprenticed in April 1803 to learn tinplate work.

Daniels, Mr. Peddled for R & B Wilcox in the South.

Daniels, William. Mentioned in John Hubbard's account books.

Darling, Luther. Peddled for R & B Wilcox in the South.

Deming, Horace. (1788—1845) Berlin tinner and son of John.

Deming, John. (1769—1800) Berlin tinner.

Deming, John. Berlin area tinner who worked for R & B Wilcox in the South during 1820s.

Deming, John & Chauncey. Farmington merchants, originally from Plainfield, who imported large quantities of tinplate.

Dickenson, Ashbel (circa 1793—1879). New Britain tinner who engaged in the tin and stove business at New Britain, CT, Richmond, VA, and Brattleboro, VT.

Dickenson, Henry Lyman (1826—1888). East Berlin tinner.

Dickenson, Jabish. Mentioned in Jedediah North's account books of 1820 to 1822.

Dickenson, Jalon. (1800—1869) Wethersfield tinner.

Dickenson, John. Mentioned in Jedediah North's account books of 1820 to 1822.

Dickenson, Josiah. Had been apprenticed to Sylvester Wilcox and operated the Palmyra, NY shop in 1822.

Dickenson, Russel (1794—1881). Berlin tinner. Mentioned in John Hubbard's account book.

Dickenson, William (1737—1806). Rocky Hill tinner.

Dobson, Isaac. Berlin tinner in the 1830s.

Dunham, Albert. (b. 1800) Berlin tinner.

Dunham, Austin. Berlin tinner mentioned in 1895 Berlin News article *Recollections of Berlin.*

Dunham, John. Berlin tinner and japanner.

Dunham, Solomon (1732—1811). Berlin tinner.

Eddy, Jesse. Berlin tinner.

Ehle, Mr. Peddler for R & B Wilcox in the South.

Evans, Robert. Peddler for John Hubbard.

Filley, Oliver. Bloomfield tinner. Purchased tinplate from Pattison & Peck.

Flagg, Allen. Mentioned in Jedediah North's account books of 1820 to 1822.

Flagg, Josiah. Mentioned in Jedediah North's account books of 1820 to 1822.

Foster, Ira. Bought tinplate from Pattison & Peck.

Galpin, Nevil. Mentioned in John Hubbard's account books.

Galpin, Silas. (b. 1786) Peddled for R & B Wilcox in the South.

Gilbert, Charles. Mentioned in Jedediah North's account books of 1820 to 1822.

Gilbert, David. Berlin tinner who bought tinplate from Pattison and Peck.

Gilbert, Mr. Tinman for R & B Wilcox in the South. Richard Wilcox felt he was one of his best workman.

Gilbert, Samuel. Berlin tinner who signed the 1813 pricing agreement.

Goodrich, Asaph. Bought tinplate from Pattison & Peck.

Goodrich, John Jr. (1776—1858) Berlin tinner and son of John Sr.

Goodrich, John Sr. (1734—1816) Berlin tinner who signed the 1813 pricing agreement.

Goodrich, Samuel. (Middletown) Mentioned in Jedediah North's account books of 1820 to 1822.

Goodrich, Seth. Berlin tinner in the 1830s.

Goodrich, Walter. (1802—1869) Berlin tinner who moved to Stevens Plains, ME.

Graves, George. Mentioned in Jedediah North's account books of 1820 to 1822.

Gregory, Alfred. Mentioned in Jedediah North's account books of 1820 to 1822.

Gregory, Elnathan. Mentioned in Jedediah North's account books of 1820 to 1822.

Hale, Joel. Mentioned in John Hubbard's account books.

Hall, Avery. Meriden tinner.

Hall, Pitkin G. Mentioned in John Hubbard's account books.

Hart, Levi. Mentioned in Jedediah North's account books of 1820 to 1822.

Haskill, John. Bought tinplate from Pattison & Peck.

Hastings, Ira. Employed by J & E North Co.

Hendrix, Mr. Peddled for R & B Wilcox in the South.

Hinsdale, J & D. Mentioned in Jedediah North's account books of 1820 to 1822.

Holister, Salmon. Mentioned in Jedediah North's account books of 1820 to 1822.

Holmes, Mr. Peddled for R & B Wilcox in the South.

Howard, Freeman. Bought tinplate from Pattison & Peck.

Hubbard, George. Peddler for R & B Wilcox in their Richmond, VA business.

Hubbard, Harvey. (1782—1863) Mentioned in John Hubbard's account books. Was still peddling in 1830.

Hubbard, John. Berlin tinner.

Hubbard, Lawrence. Peddled for R & B Wilcox in the South.

Hubbard, Lemuel. Mentioned in Jedediah North's account books of 1820 to 1822.

Hubbard, Roswell. Mentioned in John Hubbard's account books.

Hubbard & Root. Bought tinplate from Pattison & Peck.

Hunt, Robert. Mentioned in Jedediah North's account books of 1820 to 1822.

Jackson, Mr. Berlin area tinner who worked for R & B Wilcox in the South.

Jepson, James. Hartford tinner who advertised in 1768, 1769, and 1791 his tinplate work at shop opposite the Court House.

Johnson, Andrew. Mentioned in Jedediah North's account books of 1820 to 1822.

Judd, Ethan. Mentioned in Jedediah North's account books of 1820 to 1822.

Keeney, Jonathan. Middletown tinner who advertised for journeymen tinners and apprentices in 1800.

Kelsey, David. (1779—1858) Son of Enoch who advertised for tin apprentices in 1808.

Kelsey, David. (1786—1874) Son of John who was in business with his father in Winfield NY until 1822. He was also a peddler for R & B Wilcox in the South.

Kelsey, Enoch. (1753—1817) Wethersfield-Berlin tinner who advertised in 1799 for journeymen tinners and apprentices to the tin trade.

Kelsey, Israel. Mentioned in Jedediah North's account books of 1820 to 1822.

Kelsey, John. (1746—1832) Berlin tinner who moved to Winfield (Utica), NY about 1785 and continued his tin business there.

Kelsey, Samuel. (circa 1777—1816) Berlin tinner.

Kelsey, Urbani. Mentioned in Jedediah North's account books of 1820 to 1822.

Kimberly, Edward. Berlin tinner mentioned in 1895 Berlin News article *Recollections of Berlin.*

Kirby, George. Peddler for R & B Wilcox in the South. He was from Middletown. Married a Virginia girl–Elizabeth Briggs on February 18, 1822.

Lamb, James. (1777—1833) Berlin tinner.

Lamb, Lysis. (1801—1862) Berlin tinner, son of James.

Lamb & Carpenter. Berlin firm of Lysis Lamb and his brother-in-law James B. Carpenter.

Lewis, Hart. Mentioned in John Hubbard's account books.

Lewis, Mr. Peddled for R & B Wilcox in the South.

Lewis, Seth. Berlin tinner listed on tax assessment for 1797 and 1798. Bought tinplate from Pattison & Peck.

Loveland, George. Bought tinplate from Pattison & Peck.

McDonald, Mr. Peddled for R & B Wilcox in the South.

Merriam, Lauren. Meriden tinner who bought tinplate from Pattison & Peck.

Merriman, Ives. Mentioned in John Hubbard's account books.

Mildrum, Stephen. Mentioned in Jedediah North's account books of 1820 to 1822.

Mills, Charles N. Mentioned in Jedediah North's account books of 1820 to 1822.

Mills, Lewis. Mentioned in Jedediah North's account books of 1820 to 1822.

Morgan, George. Mentioned in Jedediah North's account books of 1820 to 1822.

Morton, John. Mentioned in Jedediah North's account books of 1820 to 1822.

Munson, Ransom. Peddler for John Hubbard.

Mygatt, Hiram. (1750—1836) Berlin tinner and japanner mentioned in 1895 Berlin News article *Recollections of Berlin.* Also known to have painted carriages.

Norris, Mr. Berlin area tinner who worked for R & B Wilcox in the South.

North, David. (1762—1831) Berlin tinner, son of Jedediah, who resided in Ludlow, MA in 1790. He was for a time with Linus North in Palmyra, NY but eventually settled in Meredith, NY. He later returned to Berlin.

North, Edmund. (1797—1874) In business with his brother Jedidiah.

North, Elijah. (b. 1781) Berlin trained tinner, son of Samuel, who moved to Stevens Plains ME.

North, Elijah. Mentioned in John Hubbard's account books. Probably not the Elijah North who settled in Stevens Plains, ME prior to date of these books.

North, Elisha. Brother of Elijah who went to Stevens Plains, ME to operate a tin business.

North, Jedidiah. (1789—1855) Son of Levi and founder, with his brother Edmund, of J & E North Manufacturing Co of Berlin, makers of tinman's tools.

North, Lemuel. (1786—1845) Berlin tinner, son of David.

North, Levi. (1807—1885) Employed by his brothers at J & E North Co.

North, Samuel. Berlin tinner mentioned in 1895 Berlin News article *Recollections of Berlin.*

North, Seth. (b. 1777) Berlin tinner and brother of Silas, sons of Seth Sr. He was working in Reuben North's pistol factory by 1815.

North, Silas. (1774—1839) Berlin tinner, and brother of Seth, who worked and traded in the South.

Norton, Apolles. Mentioned in John Hubbard's account books.

Norton, Isaac. Mentioned in Jedediah North's account books of 1820 to 1822.

Norton, Solomon. Bristol tinner who was originally from Berlin.

Norton, Zachariah. Bought tinplate from Pattison & Peck.

Pardy, Mr. Peddled for R & B Wilcox in the South.

Parks, Joseph S. Mentioned in Jedediah North's account books of 1820 to 1822.

Parmerly, Bani. Mentioned in Jedediah North's account books of 1820 to 1822.

Parmerly, Nathaniel. Mentioned in Jedediah North's account books of 1820 to 1822.

Pattison, Edward Sr. (circa 1720—1787) Founder of tin industry in America.

Pattison, Edward Jr. (1759—1809) Son of Edward who was also a tinner.

Pattison, Samuel. (b. 1792) Son of Shubael and also a tinner.

Pattison, Shubael. (1764—1828) Son of Edward Sr. He ran business after his father's death. He was also involved in other ventures, such as a cotton mill business with Benjamin Wilcox and the fur trade.

Pattison, William. Edward Sr's brother. A tinsmith and blacksmith.

Peck, Asahel. Bought tinplate from Pattison & Peck.

Peck, Elisha. Son-in-law of Shubael Pattison and partner in the business.

Peck, Henry. Meriden tinner.

Peck, Jabez & Oliver. Brothers who had a Berlin tin business. Purchased tinplate from Pattison & Peck.

Peck, Jesse Jr. Mentioned in Jedediah North's account books of 1820 to 1822.

Peck, Selden. Peddled for R & B Wilcox in the South.

Pettis, Simon. Mentioned in Jedediah North's account books of 1820 to 1822.

Plumb, Seth D. Meriden tinner. Bought tinplate from Pattison & Peck and tools from J & E North Co.

Pomeroy, Noah. Meriden tinner.

Porter, Edwin. Mentioned in John Hubbard's account books.

Ramsey, Selden. Peddler for John Hubbard.

Reed, Luke. Berlin tinner who bought tinplate from Pattison & Peck, and sold to John Hubbard.

Richardson, Mr. Peddled for R & B Wilcox in the South.

Roberts, John. Mentioned in Jedediah North's account books of 1820 to 1822.

Root, Mr. Peddled for R & B Wilcox in the South.

Roys, Franklin. In business of making tinman's tools with Lyman Wilcox.

Rush, Stephen N. Mentioned in John Hubbard's account books.

Sanford, Lyman. (1784—after 1850) Berlin tinner who worked for R & B Wilcox in the South. Richard Wilcox said Sanford was one of his best workman.

Savage, Jamin. Peddled for R & B Wilcox in the South.

Savage, Seth. Peddled for R & B Wilcox in the South.

Savage, William. Mentioned in Jedediah North's account books of 1820 to 1822.

Sheppard, Nab. Peddled for R & B Wilcox in the South.

Skinner, Thomas. Mentioned in Jedediah North's account books of 1820 to 1822.

Smith, J. B. Peddled for R & B Wilcox in the South.

Smith, Noah. Mentioned in Jedediah North's account books of 1820 to 1822.

Smith, Seth. Mentioned in Jedediah North's account books of 1820 to 1822.

Spenser, Matthew. Mentioned in Jedediah North's account books of 1820 to 1822.

Stocking, Daniel. Apprentice of Benjamin Wilcox. Settled in Cincinnati, Ohio area and made lamps that burned grease.

Summer, John. (Middletown) Mentioned in Jedediah North's account books of 1820 to 1822.

Summers, Joseph. Mentioned in John Hubbard's account books.

Tisdale, Riley. Bought tinplate from Pattison & Peck.

Tomson, Mr. Peddled for R & B Wilcox in the South.

Topless, Samuel. Mentioned in Jedediah North's account books of 1820 to 1822.

Tubbs, Mr. Peddled for R & B Wilcox in the South.

Ward, Truman. Peddled for R & B Wilcox in the South.

White, Mr. Peddled for R & B Wilcox in the South.

Whiting, Mr. Peddled for R & B Wilcox in the South.

Wilcox, Alfred. Mentioned in the Wilcox letters. Employed for a time by J & E North Co. Married Samuel Kelsey's daughter Miranda.

Wilcox, Allen. Berlin tinner.

Wilcox, Benjamin. (1782–1843) Middletown tinner. With his brother Richard formed company R & B Wilcox. Had a wintertime business in Virginia. Supplier to John Hubbard. Was in the cotton mill business with Shubael Pattison.

Wilcox, Daniel. (b. 1785) Brother of Benjamin. He resided in Deerfield, NY.

Wilcox, Ebenezer. Mentioned in Jedediah North's account books of 1820 to 1822.

Wilcox, Elijah. Mentioned in Jedediah North's account books of 1820 to 1822.

Wilcox, Erastus. Mentioned in Jedediah North's account books of 1820 to 1822.

Wilcox, Giles. Mentioned in Jedediah North's account books of 1820 to 1822.

Wilcox, Jeremiah Jr. Peddled for R & B Wilcox in the South.

Wilcox, Lyman. (b. 1783) Middletown maker of tinman's tools. Formed Roys & Wilcox Company with Franklin Roys. In 1844 bought the old cotton mill that Benjamin Wilcox and Shubael Pattison had operated, and manufactured their tools there.

Wilcox, Richard. (1780—1839). Owner with his brother in R & B Wilcox Company.

Wilcox, Samuel C. (1811—1886) Son of Benjamin. Became president of Roys & Wilcox Company, which continued until 1870. He was responsible for merging three rival companies together into the Peck, Stow & Wilcox Company which manufactured tinner's tools and machines, and also mechanic's tools.

Wilcox, Sylvester. (1788—1854) Brother of Benjamin and was a tinner who settled in Rome, NY. He ran a shop in Palmyra, NY about 1822. By 1831 he was also in the stove business.

Williams, Joshua. Mentioned in Jedediah North's account books of 1820 to 1822.

Williams, Mr. Berlin area tinner who worked for R & B Wilcox in the South.

Williams, Richard. Wethersfield tinner who ran a notice in July 1797 for a runaway apprentice in tinplate work.

Williams, Samuel. Bought tinplate from Pattison & Peck.

Williams, Smith. Berlin tinner who bought tinplate from Pattison & Peck.

Winchell, Mr. Peddled for R & B Wilcox in the South.

Woodruff, Cyrus. Bought tinplate from Pattison & Peck.

Woodruff, Ezekiel. Mentioned in Jedediah North's account books of 1820 to 1822.

Woodruff, Harris. Mentioned in Jedediah North's account books of 1820 to 1822.

Woodruff, Reuben. Mentioned in Jedediah North's account books of 1820 to 1822.

Yale, Charles. (1790—1834) Meriden tinner and brother of Samuel. In tin and Britannia ware business with brother Selden in Richmond, VA.

Yale, Ivah. (b. 1792) Meriden tinner and brother of Samuel.

Yale, Samuel. (b. 1787) Meriden tinner. Operated business in the Connecticut business with brothers William and Ivah.

Yale, Selden. (1795—1823) Meriden tinner and brother of Samuel. Operated business in Richmond, VA with brother Charles.

Yale, Welcome. Peddler for John Hubbard.

Yale, William. Meriden tinner and brother of Samuel.

APPENDIX G
GLOSSARY

Asphaltum: A refined form of the petroleum derivative asphalt. It is mixed with a varnish medium and used as a background coating. It is semi-transparent and produces an amber color when applied to shiny tin. Asphaltum darkens considerably with age, and few original pieces found today demonstrate the color as it was when first applied. This darkening will also affect the design colors, causing them to appear darker than they may really be due to their own aging processes.

Candy-striping strokes: The term generally refers to overtone S-strokes on a painted band. They are in a nearly straight vertical position, and usually in two alternating colors. The result is that of the type of striping on candy canes or barber poles.

Chevron strokes: Groups of strokes arranged in V-formation. They may be used as overtone strokes on a painted band, or as border strokes along the front edge of a trunk lid.

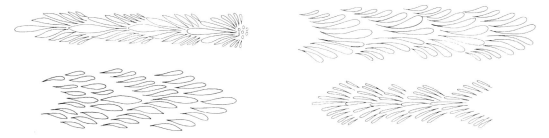

Cobra stroke: An overtone stroke on red painted units found in some Berlin area designs. The stroke is made up of a broad head and undulating tail that diminishes in width to its end. This stroke resembles the coiled cobra used by snake charmers.

Crystallized tin: A technique of treating a clean, warm, shiny tin surface with muriatic acid, sulphuric acid and water. This produces spangles on the tin surface that will sparkle when the asphaltum or colored varnish is applied over it.

Fingering technique: A painting process whereby the sharp edge of a color is softened out by dabbing it with a finger at the time of application. Fingerprints are readily visible when this technique has been used.

Hash marks or hash lines: Small accent marks, usually in groups of two or three, that are positioned on stems of flowers or the base of leaflet groups.

Ladle stroke: A brushstroke with a long arched tail. The stroke resembles a soup ladle in side view. This stroke is often found on pieces from the Stephen North shop. A larger version of it can be found on some pieces from Berlin, CT.

Lattice fence stroke: Half-circle loops, which may or may not be slightly overlapping, that are painted with thin lines. Usually in yellow, they are positioned on a stripe line or edging a painted band. They may also have a teardrop-shaped stroke at the points where they join.

Mottled asphaltum: A mottled asphaltum background is a form of graining used on country painted tinware. It is accomplished by an additional application of asphaltum gently dabbed on, or sometimes dabbed and slightly dragged, with a wide irregularly edged brush. The dabbing is placed at intervals and may run horizontally, vertically, or diagonally. The mottling will cover the entire piece of tinware excepting the bottom.

Ribbon stroke: A type of elongated border stroke that resembles a twisted ribbon.

Rick rack stroke: A variation of the ribbon stroke, but it is painted with each ribbon twist much closer together. Rick rack is sometimes found to be painted with very small, as well as tightly packed, strokes. The term rick rack has been coined from the sewing ribbon used by seamstresses.

Rope stroke: A stroke most often used for borders and made up of S-shaped strokes which connect to each other. The result gives the appearance of a twisted rope or cable. These strokes are often very broad.

S stroke: A single brushstroke shaped like the letter S. It may be very curved or it may be elongated to the point of being almost straight.

Semi-impasto painting: A technique produced by a thick painting, and not ordinarily found on country painted pieces. The process, which results in a relief or dimensional look to the strokes, is accomplished by the use of a heavier paint medium.

Wet painted technique: A painting technique that incorporates the use of two colors loaded onto the paintbrush at one time. The unit is painted on the tin with this mixture, and the two distinct colors are easily apparent. The unit is not worked over as that would cause the two colors to mix together (Refer to Fig. 1.14). This technique is not commonly found in country painting.

BIBLIOGRAPHY

BOOKS:

Adams, Charles Collard. *Middletown Upper Houses.* 1908.

Andrews, A. H. *Genealogical History of John and Mary Andrews.* Chicago IL: A. H. Andrews & Co., 1872.

Andrews, Alfred. *Genealogical History of Deacon Stephen Hart And His Descendants.* New Britain, CT: Austin Hart Esq., 1875.

Andrews, Henry Porter. *The Descendants of John Porter of Windsor Connecticut.* Saratoga Springs: G. W. Ball & Job Printer, 1893.

Barbour, Lucius B. *Families of Early Hartford, Connecticut.* Baltimore, MD: Genealogical Publ. Co. Inc., 1982.

Bickford, Christopher P. *Farmington In Connecticut.* Canaan, NH: Phoenix Publishing, 1982.

Brainard, Gilbert, and Torrey. *The Gilbert Family, Descendants of Thomas Gilbert 1582—1659.* New Haven, CT, 1953.

Brainard, Warren C. *Some Tales of Southington, as told by Mrs. R. E. Upson.* Southington, CT: Prince Publishing CO., 1935.

Brandegee, Miss Emily S. *Historical Papers — Berlin, Connecticut.* Privately published, 1928.

Brazer, Esther Stevens. *Early American Decoration.* Springfield, MA: Pond-Ekberg, 1940.

Camp, David N. *History of New Britain With Sketches of Farmington And Berlin CT 1640—1889.* New Britain, CT: William B. Thomson & Co., 1889.

Carl, Crispin, and Shipman. *The Shipman Family In America.* Published by The Shipman Historical Society, 1962.

Case, Lafayette Wallace. *The Goodrich Family In America.* Chicago, IL: Fergus Printing Co.. 1889.

Christensen, Erwin O. *Early American Designs— Toleware.* New York and London, 1952.

Christensen, Erwin O. *The Index of American Design.* New York, NY: McMillan Co., 1950.

Cist, Charles. *Sketches and Statistics of Cincinnati In 1851.* Cincinnati, OH: William H. Moore & Co., 1851.

Clark, Maryjane. *An Illustrated Glossary of Decorated Antiques from the Late 17th Century to the Early 20th Century.* Rutland VT: Charles E. Tuttle Co., 1972.

Claypool, E. A. and A. Clizbee. *A Genealogy of the Descendants of William Kelsey.* New Haven, CT: Tuttle, Morehouse & Taylor Co., 1929.

Clouette, Bruce and Roth, Matthew. *Bristol Connecticut, A Bicentennial History 1785—1985.* Canaan, NH: Phoenix Publishing, 1985.

Coffin, Margaret. *The History and Folklore of American Country Tinware 1700—1900.* Camden, NJ: Thomas Nelson & Son, 1968.

Coffin, Margaret and Charles. *Painted Tinware We've Seen.* Two Volumes. Galway, NY: Bird and Battle Publishing, 1974.

Cooke, Raeola Ford. *John Wilcox And Some Descendants of Hartford And Middletown Connecticut.* Published privately, 1987/8.

Cowles, Col. Calvin Duvall. *The Cowles Families In America* Volume I. New Haven, CT: Tuttle, Morehouse & Taylor Co., 1929.

Day, Edward Warren. *One Thousand Years of Hubbard History — 1866 To 1895.* New York, NY: Harlan Page Hubbard, 1895.

Deming, Judson Keith. *Genealogy of the Descendants of John Deming of Wethersfield, Connecticut.* Dubuque, IO: Mathis-Mets Co., 1904.

DeVoe, Shirley. *The Art of the Tinsmith, English and American.* Exton, PA: Schiffer Publishing Ltd, 1981.

DeVoe, Shirley. *The Tinsmiths of Connecticut.* Middletown, CT: Wesleyan University Press, 1968.

Dreppard, Carl. *The Primer of American Antiques.* Garden City, NY, 1944.

Dunham, Isaac Watson. *Dunham Genealogy.* Norwich, CT: Bulletin Print, 1907.

Dwight, Timothy. *Travels in New England and New York.* Volume II. Paternoster Row England: William Baynes and Son, 1823. (State Archives, Connecticut State Library, Hartford, CT)

Finney, Howard Sr. *Finney—Phinney Families In America.* Richmond, VA: The William Byrd Press, Inc., 1957.

Gillespie, C. Bancroft. *An Historic Record and Pictorial Description of the Town of Meriden Connecticut and Men Who Have Made It.* Meriden, CT: Journal Publishing Company, 1906.

Goodrich, Rev. Hiram P. *The Goodrich Family Memorial.* Part I.

Gould, Mary Earle. *Antique Tin and Tole Ware, Its History and Romance.* Rutland, VT: Charles E. Tuttle Co., 1958.

Horning, Clarence. *Treasury of American Design.* Two Volumes. New York, NY: Harry N. Abrams, Inc., 1972.

Hutchings, Dorothy. *A Quarter Century of Decorating and Teaching Country Painting.* Privately published, 1975.

Kauffman, Henry. *Pennsylvania Dutch American Folk Art.* New York, NY: Dover Publications, 1964.

Kendall, Edward Augustus. *Travels Through the Northern Parts of the United States in the Years 1807 and 1808.* Volume I. New York, NY: I. Riley, 1809. (State Archives, Connecticut State Library, Hartford, CT)

Lea, Zilla. *The Ornamented Tray—Two Centuries of Ornamented Trays (1720—1920).* Rutland, VT: Charles E. Tuttle Co., 1971.

Lipman, Jean. *American Folk Art Decoration.* New York, NY: Dover Publications, 1972.

Lipman, Jean. *American Folk Decoration.* New York, NY: Oxford University Press, 1951.

Lipman, Jean. *The Flowering of American Folk Art.* New York, NY: Viking Press, 1974.

Lord, Priscilla Sawyer and Foley, Daniel J. *The Folk Arts and Crafts of New England.* Philadelphia and New York: Chilton Books, 1965.

Menchinton, W. E. *The British Tinplate Industry.* Oxford England: Clarendon Press, 1957.

Meyers, Doris Vroom. *Berlin: Other Times, Other Voices.* Published by Berlin Free Library.

McClinton, Katherine Morrison. *A Handbook of Popular Antiques.* New York, NY: Bonanza Books, 1945.

North, Catherine. *History of Berlin, Connecticut.* New Haven CT: Tuttle Morehouse and Taylor Co., 1916.

North, Dexter. *John North of Farmington Connecticut And His Descendants.* Washington, DC, 1921.

Pattison, Kenneth Manning. *A Family Chronicle 1480—1992.* Canada: Pattison Ventures Ltd., 1992.

Peck, Ira B. *A Genealogical History of the Descendants of Joseph Peck.* Boston: Alfred Mudge & Son, 1868.

Polley, Robert. *America's Folk Art — Treasures of American Folk Arts and Crafts in Distinguished Museums and Collections.* New York, NY: G. P. Putnam's Sons, 1968.

Powers, Beatrice Farnsworth and Floyd, Olive. *Early American Decorated Tinware.* New York, NY: Hastings House, 1957.

Ramsey, Natalie Allen, editor. *The Decorator Digest.* Rutland, VT: Charles E. Tuttle Co., 1965.

Ritter, Kathy A. *Apprentices of Connecticutt 1637—1900.* Salt Lake City, UT: Ancestry Printing, 1986.

Robacker, Earl F. *Touch of the Dutchland.* New York, NY: A. S. Barnes and Co., 1965.

Sheppard, Caroleen Beckley. *The Descendants of Richard Beckley of Wethersfield, Connecticut.* Hartford, CT: The Connecticut Historical Society, 1948.

Slayton, Mariette Paine. *Early American Decorating Techniques.* New York, NY: The MacMillan Company, 1972.

Smith, Dr. Elinor V. *Descendants of Nathaniel Dickenson.* Rich Lithograph Company, 1978.

Trumbull, J. Hammond. *Memorial History of Hartford County 1633—1884* Volume II. Boston, MA: E. L. Osgood, 1886.

Upson Family Association of America. *The Upson Family In America.* New Haven, CT: Tuttle, Morehouse & Taylor Co., 1940.

Upson, Helen Rena. *The Odyssey of A Connecticut Family In Pursuit of the American Dream — An Intimate Nineteenth Century History Through the Actual Experiences of the Nine Sons of Asahel And Lydia Upson.* San Diego, CA, 1989.

Wallace, Willard M. *An Historical Sketch of Berlin Connecticut,* 1985.

Williams, C. S. *Cincinnati Directory and Business Advisor.* Cincinnati OH: C. S. Williams, 1849/50, 1851/52, 1860, 1866, and 1886.

Yale, Elihu. *The Yale Family or the Descendants of David Yale.* New Haven: Storer and Stone, 1850.

MANUSCRIPTS:

Aaron Butler Will and Inventory, 1860. (Greene County Surrogate Court, Catskill, NY). #23-676

Albert North Will and Inventory, 1850. (Otsego County Surrogate Court, Cooperstown, NY).

Edward Pattison Will and Inventory, 1788. (Connecticut State Library, Hartford, CT). L251.19.0

Elisha Peck Account Book, 1815—1818. (Connecticut Historical Society Library, Hartford, CT).

Jedediah North Day Book, 1820—1822. (Connecticut Historical Society Library, Hartford, CT).

John Hubbard Account Books, 1818—1822. (Connecticut Historical Society Library, Hartford, CT).

Kaplan, Diane E. *Robert E. Upson Family Papers.* (Yale University Sterling Memorial Library, Manuscripts and Archives). MS 1578

Kern, Laura. *Berlin Ct: What Is Special About It?* (Berlin Historical Society material at Berlin Peck Memorial Library, Berlin, CT).

Lardner Deming Account Book, 1801—1832. (State Archives, Connecticut State Library, Hartford, CT). 974.62 B45d.

New Britain Land Records

North Family of Berlin, CT Correspondence 1821—1845. (State Archives, Connecticut State Library, Hartford, CT). 920.N812

Samuel Hart Account Book, 1805—1828. (State Archives, Connecticut State Library, Hartford, CT). 974.62 B45ha.

U. S. Census of Manufacturers for Connecticut, 1820. (Connecticut State Library, Hartford, CT)

U. S. Census of Population for Cincinnati, OH, 1850.

U. S. Industrial Census for Ohio, 1850 and 1870.

Wilcox Letters, 1817—1831. (Berlin Historical Society material at Berlin Peck Memorial Library, Berlin, CT).

PERIODICALS:

Connecticut Courant Newspaper, various issues. (Connecticut State Library, Hartford, CT).

DeVoe, Shirley Spaulding, 'The Upson Tin and Clock Shop', *The Connecticut Historical Society Bulletin,* Vol. XXVI, July 1961.

Kline, Priscilla Carrington, 'New Light on the Yankee Peddler', *New England Quarterly* Vol. XII, March 1939

INDEX

Astor, John Jacob 4
Baltimore, MD . . . . . *xvi, xviii,* 4, 10
Barnum, P. T. . . . . *xviii*
Barter . . . . *xviii*
Beckley, Orin 1, 4, 5
Berlin, CT. . . *x, xii, xiii, xvi, xvii, x, xx,* Chapter 1, 81, 82, 83, 88, 88, 101, 110, 118
Brandy Hill 117, 118
Buckley, Col. William 12, 15
The Butler Shop 119, 131
Butler, Aaron 118
Butler, Aaron Jr. 118
Butler, Abel 117, 118
Butler, Ann . .118, 120, 121, 122, 123, 127, 131
Butler, Barnum 118
Butler, Eliza 118
Butler, Harriet 118, 124, 125, 127, 131
Butler, Hiram 118, 124
Butler, Lewis 118
Butler, Marilla 118
Butler, Minerva . .118, 123, 127, 131
Butler, Sarah Emma 118
Carpenter, James B. 13
Clark, Patrick 1, 4, 14
Deming, Horace 12
Deming, John 10, 12
Deming, John Jr. 12
Deming, Lardner 12, 13
Deming, Roxy 12, 17
Dunham, John 1, 12, 13
Dunham, Solomon 12
Eddy, Jesse 13, 15
Filley, Augustus 12
Flowering . . . .*xix*
Fly Creek, NY .*xiii, xvi,* 7, 81, 82, 83
Furs 4
Galpin, Norris 8
Greenleaf, Sarah 56, 57, 58
Greenville, NY . . . . . .*xiii, xvi,* 117, 118, 119, 120
Hubbard, John . . . .*xiii,* 1, 10, 12, 13, 15, 56
Japanning . . . .*xix,* 12, 57
Kelsey, Samuel 1, 14

Lacquer . . . .*xix*
Lamb, James 13, 15
Lamb, Lorenzo 13
Lamb, Lysis 13
Marion, CT . . . .*xii,* 55, 56
Miller, John 118
The North Shop 82, 83, 85, 88
North, Albert 7, 94
North, Almira 82
North, Ceylon 82
North Co., J. & E. 7, 14, 15, 81
North, Emily 82
North, Hepzibah 82
North, Jedediah 83
North, Levi 81, 83
North, Linus 81, 82
North, Mary 82
North, Mercy 83, 84, 89, 90, 90, 92, 93, 94, 95, 96, 97, 98
North, Orrin 82
North, Sarah 62
North, Simeon 81
North, Stephen . . .81, 82, 83, 94, 101
North, Stephen Jr. 82
North, Susannah 82
Otis, NY 56
Palmyra, NY . . . .*xvi,* 12
Pattison, Anna 2
Pattison, Chloe 4, 5
Pattison, Edward . . . . . *xvii,* 1, 2, 3, 5, 6, 7, 15, 43
Pattison, Edward Jr. 3
Pattison, Harriet 4, 5
Pattison, Jennie 2
Pattison, Noah 2
Pattison, Samuel 1, 4
Pattison, Shubael 1,3, 4, 5, 11, 13, 14, 15
Pattison, William 2
Peck, Elisha 4
Peddlers. . . . .*xiii, xvii, xviii, xix,* 2, 4, 7, 8, 9, 10, 11, 12, 13, 14, 16, 56, 118
Petersburg, VA . . . . .*xvi,* 7, 8, 10, 12
Pierson, Alanson 82, 83
Pontypool, Wales . . . . .*ix, xvii, xix*
Porter, Abel 13

Porter, Linus 13
Porter, Samuel III 3
Richmond, VA . . . .*xvi,* 7, 14
Rome, NY . . . .*xvi,* 11, 12
Scutt, Eli 118
Tin industry, origins . *xvii, xix,* 1, 16
Tole, toleware . . . .*viii*
Truck . . . .*xviii*
The Upson Shop 58, 65, 67, 80
Upson, Asahel 55, 56, 57, 58
Upson, Dewitt 56
Upson, Elliot 56
Upson, Gad Ely 56
Upson, James 55
Upson, James Robert 56, 57
Upson, Josiah 55, 57
Upson, Lauren 56
Upson, Robert Ellsworth 57, 58
Upson, Salmon 55, 56, 57, 58
Upson, Warren 56
Utica, NY 11
Varnish . . . .*xix,* 82
Wilcox, Benjamin 1, 5, 6, 7, 8, 9, 11, 12, 14
Wilcox, Daniel 12
Wilcox, Hepzibah 8
Wilcox, Richard 6, 8, 12, 14
Wilcox, Samue l6
Wilcox, Sylvester 6, 11
R. & B. Wilcox & Co. 7, 11, 12, 15
Winchell, George D. 57
Yale, Charles 14
Yale, Ivah 14
Yale, Samuel 14
Yale, Samuel Jr. 14
Yale, Selden 14
Yale, William 14

Maps

18th Century Tin Centers . . . . . .*xvi*
Areas of Early Tin Businesses in Connecticut . . . .*xx*
Berlin and East Berlin, Connecticut 15